T0090172

GOD

Expelled

From America

Mirta M Signorelli

Order this book online at www.trafford.com
or email orders@trafford.com

Most Trafford titles are also available at major online book retailers.

Printed in the United States of America.

ISBN: 978-1-4269-3466-7 (sc)

ISBN: 978-1-4269-3467-4 (hc)

ISBN: 978-1-4269-3452-0 (e-book)

Library of Congress Control Number: 2010908819

*Our mission is to efficiently provide the world's finest, most comprehensive book publishing
service, enabling every author to experience success. To find out how to publish your
book, your way, and have it available worldwide, visit us online at www.trafford.com*

Trafford rev. 7/8/2010

 www.trafford.com

North America & international
toll-free: 1 888 232 4444 (USA & Canada)
phone: 250 383 6864 ♦ fax: 812 355 4082

Eternal God.

Eternal God, the light of the minds that know You,

The life of the souls that love You.

The strength of the wills that serve You.

Help us to know You so that we may truly love You.

To love You so that we may fully serve You.

Whom to serve is perfect freedom.

(Gelasius Prayer Book)

THE TEN COMMANDMENTS

1. You Shall Have No Other Gods Before Me.

2. You Shall Not Make For Yourself An Idol.

3. You Shall Not Take The Lord's Name In Vain.

4. Remember The Sabbath Day And Keep It Holy.

5. Honor Your Father And Your Mother.

6. You Shall Not Murder.

7. You Shall Not Committ Adultery.

8. You Shall Not Steal.

9. You Shall Not Bear False Witness.

10. You Shall Not Covet.

What Are They?

The Ten Commandments, or Decalogue, are a list of religious and moral imperatives that, according to the <u>Hebrew Bible</u>, were spoken by <u>God</u> to the <u>people of Israel</u> from <u>Mount Sinai</u> and later authored by God and given to <u>Moses</u> in the form of two stone tablets. They are recognized as a moral foundation in <u>Judaism</u>, <u>Christianity</u> and <u>Islam</u> religions.

America, from its inception, has used the bible as a guidebook for moral human behavior. The Ten Commandments were utilized by most of the original colonies to formulate their basic justice system. God does not give us the liberty to behave as we please. Serious consequences on society and self occur when His laws are violated.

The Ten Commandments are the backbone of all inspired words of God. Yet, secularism is trying to "break the backbone" of this great country by chipping away at their importance in today's society. Will God still bless a nation where its citizens no longer honor his laws? Time will be our judge.

DEDICATION

This book is lovingly dedicated to God, the Father of all Creation. To Jesus Christ, the Alpha and Omega, and to my Inspirer and Encourager, the Holy Spirit. My deepest gratitude for walking with me through the fire and covering me with Your grace. Thank You for allowing me to participate in the sacred work of Your Kingdom. This book is also dedicated to all my heavenly angels. In addition, I would like to thank all my earthly angels who offered me continued support during one of the most difficult times in my life, for they believed in me and affirmed my journey with their trust. Yes, many earthly angels along my journey of life have been like "beacons of light", shinning in the dark sea of life. They have given me encouragement and support when I could no longer see the "light at the end of the tunnel." Because of them, this book has become a reality. The goal of this book is to reveal the "Truth" in our society. This book will cause controversy and will be denied by some. Nevertheless, the words have been spoken and it is up to our society to make the next move.

CONTENTS

PREFACE

God has been expelled from America. I believe that there is a hidden agenda to remove God from our government, schools, media, and even our books. Children are allowed to study Darwanism in school, but it becomes illegal to study intelligent design. Think about it, prayer is forbidden in schools. It's happy holidays not Merry Christmas, Nativity scenes are banned from public property, along with the Ten Commandments, the foundation on which our nation was built, has been forcibly removed by court order from many public institutions. However, I'm not the only one noticing this, as a matter of fact, if you have watched the Fox News Channel recently, it becomes increasingly obvious that there are many concerned Christians in America today who feel the same way that I do.

Yet, we the people of God have remained silent for too long. Due to our silence, we have given rise to atheists and special interest groups, who have accelerated a frontal attack on God. For example, it was around the Thanksgiving holiday of 2009 where statements such as, "No God, No Problem", and "Yes, Virginia, There is No God" appeared on billboards and on sides of busses. America received a powerful frontal attack against God by an athiest special interest group. Not only did the group not deny their advertisements, they took pride in them, making sure they were aired them during the Christmas season. Currently, another atheist special interest group is trying to re-write some of the children's school books to make them more "inclusive" by eliminating any reference to God or the Bible.

As this book goes to press in Pensacola, Florida, Liberty Counsel has filed a comprehensive lawsuit against the Santa Rosa County

School District and its Superintendent, Timothy S. Wyrosdick, for persistent violations against the First Amendment rights. The lawsuit that has been filed is on behalf of two dozen citizens, which includes teachers, students, staff, parents, volunteers, local members of the community and even former students of the school. The complaints are that students can no longer say "God Bless", teachers must hide in their closets to pray, there can be no student initiated prayers or off the clock religious discussion among adults. Furthermore, Christian groups cannot rent school facilities for private religious functions, even if it is for the benefit of the students. The Santa Rosa School District has decided to pay the ACLU $200,000 in legal fees. I wonder if that money came from the taxpayers? It is clear to see that the ACLU is making a mockery of the First Amendment. As the banning of Bible truth in America continues, we will continue to see the rise of such athiest groups and individuals that will foster an acceptance of moral decay in our nation. What was once called "sin" is now called "choice" and public or secular life is strictly based on "political correctness" alone.

Of course, we see that contempt for the Laws of God is deliberate in the entertainment industry. Widely promoted are the pleasure seeking sins such as sex, pornography, violence and drug use which has become an accepted form of entertainment. As the youth of America are being bombarded with immoral images, the line between right and wrong is not being defined in our society, and the results are school violence, teen pregnancies, drugs, alcohol, and abuse in the family.

We are living in a period of moral darkness and decline, however, our society can obtain victory over sin and evil by adhering to God's Law. For it is by the power of the Holy Spirit that we gain victory over sin, and we begin to experience life "more abundantly." But first the light of God's Word must shine into our moral darkness, and since God is faithful, He will forgive our sins and cleanse our society from all unrighteousness, so that the people who are separated from God will be forgiven and hope will be restored.

Unfortunately, Satan has not only succeeded in removing the Laws that would restore our national morality, the Ten Commandments, from our government, but he has also been successful in removing them from the hearts of many Christians. Such people become spiritually dead and once the person is spiritually dead, then separation between God and man has occurred, at which point man will be capable of unspeakable crimes and actions against God and each other.

It is fair to say that every person who has ever lived, with the exception of Jesus Christ, has broken the Ten Commandments at one time or another. The act of "sin" is a transgression against the Law of God. And the Law of God, my friends, is a reflection of God's love and care towards man. You see, God knew that only by following His laws was mankind going to be capable to reach it's full potential. For example, approximately 3,500 years ago God was opposed to murder, stealing, and adultery just to name a few, now, do you think that such sins still offend Him today? Of course they do, because God is consistent. God is the same today as He was in the beginning of time. We are the ones who keep changing the rules of the game. There are so many conflicting convictions within the Christian community today, that everyone seems to be making up their own personal moral codes, basically their own Ten Commandments.

In our current society, there seems to be a low regard for God's Law or the Ten Commandments, and this can only lead me to believe that, "currently there is a low regard for God in general." This is precisely why this book has been written, to open the eyes and minds of the public.

For those who know me, know that I have had many experiences in my life, that shaped my spiritual character. I was born in 1954 in Camaguey, Cuba. Being Hispanic, and from a religious family, I attended church regularly. I lived in the small little town of Pina in Camaguey, Cuba for the first five years of my life. Nearly all of life's activities revolved around the activities of the parish church. It seems that there was always something going on at church. Whether it was Sunday's service, weddings, church fairs, parish school events, and even funerals, kept the small community busy and in touch with each other. Then came Fidel Castro with his communist regime which changed everything in the small town. There would be no more "Church Services" or any other kind of church affair without the approval of the military. My father and mother, were detained and taken as prisoners for working against the Castro regime. I still can remember today looking through a large bob-wire fence to get a glimpse of my parents in jail. It was during that time that my mother gave birth to my sister. Almost immediately after my sister's birth, my father was able to obtain the appropriate paper work to come to the United States. God had answered our prayers! Unfortunately, they could not get the paperwork for my sister since she had just been born, so she was left with my grandparents in Cuba. It took seven long years for the family to become reunited again here in America

While in the United States, I was like many immigrant children. I could not speak the language and at times I felt depressed and anxious in this large new world. However, we were now free. Free to go to church, pray and worship God in whatever way we wanted. Whatever negative feelings I was experiencing, it was all worth it to be here, in the United States. My parents felt the same way. Although they had to leave their child, their land, and their community, they now had what they considered their basic human right, freedom to worship God.

In my early years, leading up to high school, I attended parochial and public schools. I remember having my first mystical religious experience at around age seven, then at twelve, and then at eighteen. After that, there were many more of them, spiritual in nature, but those first ones were the most significant, and marked the first milestones in my life. Each conversion or mystical experience was a "born again" experience, which for me meant an ever deeper inner commitment to a spiritual path with God. My first experience, left me with great devotion to Jesus Christ, especially for the passion of Christ. At age twelve, I had my first communion and I vowed to dedicate my life to God, and then at around eighteen, I had my first "mystical experience" following prayers, I was swept up in an exalted state of consciousness. After that, I never saw the world the same again. For me, I wanted to follow the road that great devotional masters had followed, especially, our Lord Jesus, and it began by first honoring the Ten Commandments of God. I don't want to be a hypocrite, so I will be the first to admit that I have "not" kept the ten commandments faithfully. But through the grace of Jesus Christ, I have become a spiritual warrior against sin and have been able to persevere in keeping the laws of God.

As I stated before, the removal of the Ten Commandments from the public schools had severe repercussions beyond anything that we could imagine. Basically, sin has become unidentifiable. Sin must be recognized in order for us to change negative behavior. If we can't recognize sin, then, there is no repentance or reconcilliation to God. People become free to function without restraints, without moral or decency laws, possibly plunging deeper into moral darkness, unable to seek the face of a loving and forgiving God.

As secular America continues with the campaign to remove God from the public arena, Christian churches who have been passive for many years, are now springing into action to bring awareness to this very blatant ommission of God in our country. Ultimately, it is a personal choice whether or not to obey the living God of the Ten Commandments. However, we must remember that His standards are the guidelines that our country was founded on, and the standard for our behavior. If America continues to rationalize and give in to the secularism that wants us to choose another way of life, then let me remind you what Deuteronomy 30:15-20 has to say, "See, I have set before you today life,and good, death and evil, in that I command you today to love the Lord your God, to walk in His ways, and to keep His commandments....I have set before you life and death, blessing and cursing; therefore choose life, that both you and your descendants may live that you may love the Lord your God, that you may obey His voice, and that you may cling to Him, for He is your life, and the length of your days, and that you may dwell in the land which the Lord swore to your fathers, to Abraham, Issac, and Jacob, to give to them."

So my friends, the choice is yours, and it's either life or death. God's foundational laws of righteous living given to us by the Ten Commandments actually offers us the gift of eternal life. Remember the first commandment, "I am the Lord your God, who brought you out of the house of Egypt, out of the house of bondage" (Exodus 20:2). He is first and foremost our God. He is our Creator, so we bow down to Him. Then as He commands us, "You shall have no other gods before Me" (Exodus 20:3). However, God's way is the way of love, and in order to adhere to the commandments of God, we must have faith that God will provide a way to make it possible for us to obey Him. For God, Himself said, "I will never leave you or forsake you"(Hebrews 13:5). The negative pull of this world and of human nature is much too powerful for man to overcome without God's help. In order to receive His help we must ask for it, and we ask by having faith, that He will give us His Holy Spirit to dwell within us and change the way we think, speak, and relate to the world around us. Yes, God will give us discernment and trust in Him to make the right choices and to obtain eternal life.

Let Us Pray:

Eternal Father, Sweet Majesty of the Most High. Grant this humanity the grace of a strong faith that it should contemplate Your marvelous works on earth and throughout the universe. Father, make us humble in the face of Your creations. Although we are sinful in nature, cover us with Your divine love and give us Your eternal peace. Jesus, light of humanity, come and extinguish the darkness of man, and light the candles of love in every heart. Lord Jesus, heal us and take our iniquity from us. Mend our wounds and transform our hearts so that this nation once again will bring honor and glory to Your Name. In Jesus Name we pray, Amen.

INTRODUCTION

America, from its very beginning has been the subject of praise and criticism, fascination, and misconception. Although it is hard to understand the complexity of such a great nation, America is "unlike" any other developed nation in the world. When we take a look at the morals, values, and ethics that made America the greatest nation in the world, very distinct and substantial changes are now occurring in our country today.

One of the distinguishing factors of the makeup of America is that since its conception, the freedom that Americans enjoy was derived from the Judeo/Christian faith traditions of our nation's founding fathers. Currently America is drifting away from the most basic principles, specifically, the Ten Commandments. Our ancestors could have not imagined that the "Pledge of Allegiance" could be labeled "unconstitutional" and not recited in schools by some students because it includes the words "under God." The Supreme Court banned prayer in public schools, and God has been "expelled" from politics, business, and our way of life in general. America has willfully rejected the God of the Judeo/Christian Bible as our source of divine authority, in order to be politically correct. It is correct to say that churches beliefs and their symbols do not belong in American courthouses and statehouses, but God certainly does. The United States was conceived in faith and guided by God. For it was strong faith in our Creator and reliance on Divine Providence that gave our founding fathers the wisdom and courage to create the land of the free.

Unfortunately, as America becomes more and more interested in the attributes consistent with the world of today, greed has become the substance of our egoism in this nation. While self-will, bitterness, frustration and hate, are the basic consequences of the denial of God's spiritual laws, it always leads to the destruction of the human soul. As the denial of God becomes accepted by the society as "politically correct" behavior, this lack of "spiritual accountability" has established the foundation for many of the decisions made today by our nation's leaders. For example, in 2009, the American people voted into the White House a President, who requested that Georgetown University remove all spiritual signs and symbols from their halls before he would deliver his speech to the assembly. The university willingly complied in order to have the President of the United States, deliver the address. One of the signs covered was the early Christian monogram for the name of Christ, "IHS." It seems that the President is going out of his way to make sure that the public is denied a viewing of the Christian God. Obviously, he wants secularism to be the only acceptable mode for public discourse. Georgetown, a Catholic University: "Why did you deny God in order to comply with the President's orders"? "What happened to honoring and commitment to God"? Christian belief is clear, Jesus said, "Whoever acknowledges me before men, I will also acknowledge him before my Father in heaven. But whoever disowns me before men, I will disown him before my Father in heaven"(Matthew 10:32-33).

It was in 1947 that America started its path of becoming a secular and atheist society. The United States Supreme Court with its decision on **Everson vs. Board of Education** established that the law of the land would be **separation of church and state**. Using this ruling non-believers started their attack against biblical traditions that where intertwined in public life.

The agenda of the non-believers is to remove all signs of God from America landscape and unfortunately, they have done an excellent job at it so far. In 1962, the Supreme Court ruled that prayer in public school was unconstitutional and in 1973 made abortion legal in the United States. These non-believers are presently helping to rewrite the history of America by downplaying the importance of the Judeo-Christian traditions in its creation. Please visit the following website to learn about our founding fathers faith statements http:// www.eadshome.com/QuotesoftheFounders.htm.

As the citizens of the United States become more committed to being "secularized", they have also become more pagan in their values and belief system. New Age religions and false gods and idols are now in the forefront of our society. Money is the god of many. As the bumper sticker reads, "The one with the most toys wins" seems to be our way of life. Today, the love and faith in God is substituted with the love of money and materialism. America's spending spree has escalated to the point of a national recession; bankruptcies, foreclosures, high unemployment have all become a part of our everyday life. Yes, America is facing problems of Biblical proportions; however, instead of turning to God, we find that on Sunday morning, churches across America lie half-full, as their parishioners deal with duties that are more important to them. Sunday mornings are now utilized for going out to breakfast, taking the kids to ball practice, and doing house chores early to free time up for afternoon sporting events. These tasks are more important than glorifying God.

America's freedoms were established on three documents: The Constitution, The Declaration of Independence, and the Bill of Rights. These documents are the basis of our heritage as Americans, and they are substantiated by biblical principles. When we deny God as a nation, we are in fact denying the basic principles contained in these founding documents. The results would be a deterioration of our moral fabric as a "New World" form of spirituality begins to define our nation.

A Gallop Poll in 2008 reported that Christian Americans are declining in large numbers and members are getting older. The report showed that in the first year of tracking, which was 1948, 91 percent of Americans identified themselves as Christians. In 2008, the percentage of Americans identified themselves as Christians dropped to 77 percent. Recent independent surveys reveal that the percentage of Christian Americans is at 75 percent. This rapid decrease in Americans claiming to be Christian is disturbing, and at the current rate of decline, by 2050, there will be an equal number of non-believers as believers in the Christian God. This will give the non-believers the opportunity to remove the tax exemption status from churches. Can your church remain open if they lose this benefit?

Voices against God are accepted and even encouraged, especially in the media. Case in point: Comedian Kathy Griffin said on a video in reference to accepting an award, "A lot of people come here and they thank Jesus for this award. I want you to know that the one that has less to do with this award is Jesus. He did not help me a bit. If it were up to Him, Cesar Milan would be up here with that damn dog. So stick it Jesus. This award is my God now."

America is witnessing more than religious bigotry, the secular media wrote about it on Easter 2009, as the 'Newsweek' cover story stated, "*The Decline and Fall of Christianity in America.*" As I have mentioned earlier, America is facing problems of biblical proportions, and according to 'Newsweek,' the percentage of Americans who think faith will help answer the country's current problem dipped to a historic low of 48% down from 64% in 1994. Unfortunately, as Barack Obama took office in 2009, the leadership of our country has become increasingly "secular" as America continues to shift rapidly towards a form of "liberalism" which many are calling the "new American socialism." As the third millennium approaches, it is clear that this new form of pagan spirituality is transforming our culture and leading the way for the "expulsion" of God in every aspect of our American life.

In Florida 2009, a hospital chaplain was terminated for praying in the name of Jesus Christ, a Navy chaplain was also dismissed from his duties for doing alike, and faced a court martial. An Air Force Chaplain was embroiled in charges of religious coercion after he told cadets that their first duty was to God, and he encouraged them to observe the National Day of Prayer. Currently, Air Force Chaplains are banned from using Jesus in their prayers, so are hospital and hospice chaplains in public prayer, and this list increases daily. In relation to my own personal experience, as a long time hospice chaplain, I was advised that the word "God" could not be used in organizational prayers. The following is my story, and ultimately the reason for writing this book. (The Article in the Sun Sentinel included.)

On Monday, February 23, 2009, while employed as a chaplain for a Boca Raton Hospice, I was forced to choose between God, and my job as a chaplain. During the morning meeting, the first order of business for the chaplains was the review of a letter to the spiritual care department written by the human resource director and signed by the organization's vice president. The letter specifically asked the spiritual care department to cease from using the word "God" in organizational prayers. The letter stated that chaplains needed to be more "inclusive" of the atheist or the non-believers in a group setting. My response was that I needed to obtain further clarification, since I could not do my work as a chaplain without using the word "God." "It's like telling a nurse that she cannot use her medical tools to care for the sick." "My tool is God, I stated." The word alone brings peace and comfort to all who hear His name. He (God) is the reason I am a chaplain today. God is the reason why I work with the dying, in the comforting and serving of them."

Furthermore, God is as generic as you can get. I have been a chaplain for a very long time and I understand that we have to be sensitive to the beliefs of others. I was not using denominational names such as Jesus, Abba, Allah, Jehovah, or by whatever name you should call our Creator, if you believe in a Creator. At which point a reference was made to the spiritual reflection that I presided on a couple of weeks ago. The meditation was on the Twenty Third Psalm, The Lord is My Shepherd. The department supervisor, who is not a chaplain and has no spiritual care experience, informed me that the usage of the word Lord, gave the meditation a Christian connotation. Therefore, it would be against the new organizational policy.

As a hospice chaplain for over a decade, I have had much experience working with the dying and when a person has less than six months to live, they move towards what I call, "Divine Consolation." I believe that the human mind searches for truth and knowledge of the infinite journey of life. The word "God" becomes an essential aspect of comfort care and must be used in prayers. Whether the prayer is offered in the hospice organizational setting, chapel, or the patient's home "God" should be freely said in all venues. As a chaplain, I should not be restricted in any way offering prayer to the public with five hundred people or a private prayer of only two individuals.

I must admit that I felt frustrated and alone. For it did not seem to bother the other chaplains in the room who could be "politically correct" and follow the organizational guidelines placed on them. Most being more concerned in collecting a paycheck in a bad economy than standing up for what I considered a violation of basic religious right. I wonder how many religious leaders today are willing to compromise God's laws to keep their employment.

As the news of what happened spread throughout our community, one of the local newspapers wrote an article on this incident. Immediately, the Associated Press picked up the story and it became world news. People from all over the globe were writing e-mails and letters to me, or commenting in blogs and responding to the different articles from around the world. "God is under attack," many would say. More and more people were sharing their stories of similar situations in which being **"politically correct"** was more important than acknowledging the God of Creation. Shouldn't people have the right to acknowledge God publicly in accordance to what their conscious dictates?

Unfortunately, this is not the case. There are thousands of people who have been denied the right to properly acknowledge God today, here in America, under the precept of being "politically correct." No one can make any reference to religious truth publicly without fear of retribution from the establishment, such as termination. It seems to me that this kind of all-inclusive religiosity is based upon a form of relativism directly at odds with the traditional elements of many religious faiths.

The inter-office letter that was read at the chaplains' meeting by the senior chaplain, gave us a "directive," just as the CEO described it to the reporter for the newspaper article. The organization wanted us to be more "inclusive" of the atheist or the non-believer publicly. That would mean that I would have to remove all statements from my vocabulary that acknowledges "God" publicly. I believe that such a restriction would be a violation of my basic religious right guaranteed to me by the Constitution of the United States. Unfortunately, our current president would not agree. The beliefs or opinions of religious people have no place in public, and essentially such individuals should hide their faith. A good example being the Georgetown incident, in which the President asked the university to cover all religious symbols before the date of his speaking engagement.

Currently, when it comes to the courts, they too have taken a stand against the rights of individuals who want to honor God publicly. The results have been a ban on prayer in the schools, at graduations, and displays that are religious in nature, such as the Ten Commandments monuments being on public grounds. The current trend is for justices to regulate and restrict any form of religion, which acknowledges God as the One, Supreme Creator of the Bible. The fundamental liberties of believers in God are in jeopardy with this current administration and in America in general. This already has been the case in other parts of the world, where socialistic forms of governments rule the people.

This book, my friends, is dedicated to the One True God, my Lord, Jesus Christ. We are living in perilous times. Now is the time, if you have not already done so, to begin a daily walk of prayer and meditation. Pray for all that is in your heart, but also pray for God's mercy upon this great nation of ours. George Washington once said, "It is impossible to rightly govern the world without God and the Bible. Do not ever let anyone claim to be a true American patriot if they ever attempt to separate religion from politics." What are we coming to in this great nation when the government is going out of its way to wipe out any mention or form of God? My friends, we are in the presence of a massive rejection of God and biblical spirituality. This, I believe, has brought about general confusion in the areas of spirituality, morality, and ethics in our culture, as the spread of "institutionalized paganism" continues to replace the fundamental Judeo/Christian philosophy. It is interesting that while we, in the

United States are called to be tolerant and inclusive, I would argue that behind the exhortation to inclusiveness there is a "new world" view which challenges God and His Law as we know it.

Today, God's way of life does not drive the American way of life. God's Holy name and His commandments has been stricken from our institutions of higher learning and our hallowed halls of justice. Do you remember what God said to Moses if His commandments were not respected and obeyed? "But if ye will not harken unto me, and will not do all these commandments, and if ye shall despise my statues, or if your soul abhor my judgments, so that ye will not do all my commandments, but that ye break my covenant: I also will do this unto you; I will even appoint over you terror"(Lev.26.14-16).

As God's Laws are challenged, we need to look at the sinfulness in our society, which ultimately begins in our souls. Although man is a sinner by birth, he is not held responsible for this. When man becomes a sinner by practice, then he is responsible to God and others for the sins committed. Sin is the transgression of the divine commands, specifically, the Ten Commandments. For these Ten Commandments are concerned with man's relationship with God, and the focus of these Commandments deal with the responsibilities of man to God who is both Creator and Redeemer. The Ten Commandments reflect the Divine character of God. This is true of all rules or regulations in general. For example, consider the extensive federal regulations that govern handicapped access to public buildings. What do these laws state about the society that created them? That Americans want to include the handicapped in the ordinary events of public life. You see, the law always reveals the character of the lawgiver. This was especially true at Mount-Sinai where every one of the Ten Commandments was stamped with the being and the attributes of Almighty God.

Many today are asking, "What gives God the right to tell people what to do?" Well, the preface to the Ten Commandments tells us that because God is Lord, and our God, and Redeemer, we are bound to keep all of His commandments." However, today, more people seem to be interested in finding out about God, but less willing to do what He says. They have created their own "designer" god, a god that meets their criteria. Moreover, they do this is because they do not know the God of the Bible, because if they did, they would recognize Him as the absolute authority, and respect His Laws. Respect for God always demands respect for His Laws. When people have a low regard or no regard for God, as it is evident in our culture, then what follows is a decline in morality as everyone makes up their own personal moral code as they go along.

The following chapters will focus on God's moral laws, as He expresses His perfect and righteous will for our lives. They also include what happens when sin is not restrained in our society, and when there is no accountability to God. The Ten Commandments bring a heightened sense of understanding of what God requires and forbids. However, since today our society is moving further and further away from any accountability to God, what is going to deter people from committing horribly, destructive sins which not only hurt themselves but the society in which we live in? Nothing; Without the Ten Commandments of God there is no yardstick. There is no measurement of right or wrong, society is on its own!

1

FIRST COMMANDMENT OF GOD

You Shall Have No Other Gods Before Me

"And one of them, a doctor of the law, asked him, tempting him: Master, which is the greatest commandment in the law? Jesus said to him: You shall love the Lord your God with your whole heart, with your whole soul, and with your whole mind. This is the greatest and the First Commandment. And the second is like to this: You shall love your neighbor as yourself. On these two commandments dependeth the whole law and the prophets"

(Mathew 22: 34-40).

The Ten Commandments are the core of the laws of God, these laws are universal in nature and they set a moral standard that enables humanity to know when it is drifting away. In essence, the Ten Commandments are the standard by which all human beings establish and maintain order. They are God's spiritual laws that, if not adhered to, can pose severe spiritual consequences. This being especially true in our modern day society, as each of the commandments embraces the principle of basic respect for human life.

When we look at the Ten Commandments, we see how they are disregarded today in America. For example, statements such as, "I will steal from those who really will not miss it, or "I'm not causing anyone any harm by lying on my taxes" are common today and are an expression of the belief that we are able to make up our own rules, based on our own personal preference. Essentially, we make them as we go along.

The rule of life is that each cause will bring about an effect, whether it is immediately or in the future. By obeying God's Ten Commandments humanity can be certain that the cause will produce a good and desirable effect. Unfortunately, America has moved towards a form of spirituality which I refer to as "paganism" a level above atheistic humanism, and the Ten Commandments have been expelled under the force of the politically correct group, who instead of rejecting sin, are rejecting the spiritual Laws of God.

There is a popular belief in the American society today, a belief of a "new world view" which brings with it a new form of spirituality. Americans are evoking a new religious option, "a comprehensive approach to spirituality which unites the East and the West, and thus a new technology for transformation is born". Many state that with this new spirituality, there is no room for the Ten Commandments, they are too rigid and judgmental with no room for cultural changes or raised societal consciousness. The religious consciousness of America has changed. The people not only tolerate, but also have institutionalized a politically correct system, which denies God in the public square.

In fact, the Supreme Court went against legal precedent of the past 200 years, and against the intention of the founding fathers of our nation, and banned the Ten Commandments when it appeared to be presented as a religious doctrine. The Supreme Court did say that some displays would be appropriate if they were portrayed neutrally in order to place honor on America's legal history but not God. The justices voted that in the two Kentucky Courthouses, the Ten Commandments were considered a religious display and were therefore unconstitutional. This is an interesting development of modern time, since placing the Ten Commandments in public places was a practice that was common across the first three hundred years in America beginning with the Pilgrims. In the Bible, Moses,

Deuteronomy 6:9, to display the Ten Commandments, requests us this is the only place in the Bible that requests that His people display any Scripture verse. My friends, what has happened to us? How is it that intelligent and educated people can dismiss the most important ten rules of behavior that God expects us all to follow? Regardless of faith or tradition, the Ten Commandments are laws given by God to govern the moral behavior of a society: "Do not steal, lie, commit adultery, etc. Even a religiously diverse nation, as the United States, can see the benefits of the Ten Commandments on its culture.

Conversely, is God worshipped in America today? Better yet, do people even think that He exists? Evolutionists reject the Creation account of God, and thus it becomes easy then to reject the thought of the existence of any moral laws. As America rejects the authority of God, we see the decline of basic moral values, and an increase in crime. The rejection of Christian spirituality becomes a very prevalent part of a new world view, giving rise to a post-modern world that believes that "truth" is found in power and control, and not in God or His laws.

It is clear that the existence of a personal and moral God is a fundamental belief for all Christians. For if there is no God, then there is no moral being to sin against. Therefore, salvation is not necessary. If there is no God, then there certainly would be no miracles and all those stories in the Gospel of Jesus Christ would be no more than fairy tales. So the question arises in today's society, "Does God exist"?

The argument for creation specifies that since there is a universe, then it must have been caused by something beyond itself. This is based on the law of causality, which states that every limited thing is caused by something other than itself. In order to state it simply, there are three factual statements. First, that the universe had a beginning, second, that anything that has a beginning must have been caused by something else. Thirdly, that the universe was caused by something else, and that something else is God. Essentially, all the wondrous designs in the universe imply a designer, and the greater the design the greater the designer.

Yes, friends, no doubt, that God exists and He is the God of the Bible. The argument of creation proves not only that God exists, but also that He has ultimate power over the universe. For only a God with incredible, ultimate power could create and sustain the whole universe. Not only has God caused all things, but also He holds them together, and keeps them in existence. Furthermore, God is of mighty and great intelligence. Even Carl Sagan admitted before he died that the design of the universe was far beyond anything that man could devise. God is all knowing, He knows many things that we cannot even begin to comprehend. God designed our brains; He knows the way we think and act. In the beginning, God told Moses His name and God said, "I AM WHO I AM" (Ex.3:14).

The First Commandment states, "You shall have no other gods before me" and it seems to be a simple commandment to keep, since most people do not actively worship statues of pagan gods. However, this commandment refers to "any" excessive devotion offered to anyone or anything besides God. This commandment says that it is wrong to allow any created thing, even a human being, to become more important to us than our Creator. Christians sometimes have difficulty in distinguishing between the First and the Second Commandment of God because they both relate to the worship of false gods. A good rule of thumb to follow for determining whether a passage is addressing the First or Second Commandment is that a First Commandment transgression is worshiping anything created by God, such as the moon, stars, or the sun. The Second Commandment transgression is worshiping anything that was created or formed by man; anything that man has created with his own hands and hearts and then places it before God.

On December 28, 1990, Jesus appeared to a visionary in Conyers, Georgia. I know that there will be people reading this book who will not believe this, but just hear me out. Her name was Nancy Fowler and she lived in Conyers, Georgia. Many pilgrims came on a daily basis, from as far away as Europe, to see and hear her give messages from Jesus. On that 28th day of December, Ms. Fowler stated that Jesus said to her, "I tell you, if you put anything before me, then you are in violation of My First Commandment.

For example, You overeat. You want power. You like the power. You want a lot sex. Oh, how deceived man can be by Satan. Men think that they are masters of themselves, but it is Satan who is master of them. I say, love your God with your whole heart, mind, soul, and strength. Do not love anyone or anything more than Me. If you do, you will become a slave. I alone am the Master who can set you free. Love Me and you will never be a slave. But if you love Satan, you will be in bondage." Well, I guess that says it all, man does place many things before God, money, eating, sex, power, etc. Unfortunately, the list keeps growing daily, but man continues with his excuses and does not understand the reality of evil in this world and its terrible consequences for generations to come.

When appearing on Inside Edition, Newsweek editor at large, Evan Thomas, stated that President Obama is a "brave" and "great-teacher" who "stands above everybody." In his statements Mr. Thomas flattered President Obama by saying, "I mean in a way Obama's standing above the country, above the world, he's sort of God." For some, Barak Obama has become a god in their eyes, and they seem to follow him blindly as he leads this country down a path of socialism.

Another god figure in America was Michael Jackson. At the death of Michael Jackson, more than one million people around the world applied for 17,000 free tickets to his memorial service. Organizers for the funeral in Los Angeles, said that they put together one of the largest massive security operations in history. An online lottery, for the memorial service, immediately became operational which allowed fans to watch the ceremony on big screen TV. At their local Nokia Theater, the tribute to Michael's life was streamed online and televised. Michael Jackson was not god, but he certainly had been treated and worshipped as one. Even after death, Michael is idolized and treated with more respect than God. Think about it. When was the last time that God was idolized in this country, by so many people and at one time?

Michael Jackson had unbelievable talent. He wrote, recorded, and produced music that lead to many great songs. He was a singing and dancing sensation. Michael Jackson was brilliant and he was a master showman. However, for sure, he was not God. Yet, our culture still worships and honors him as a being of greatness. Unfortunately, people seem to mistake the entertainer's talents, popularity, and success with the greatness equal to that of God. They forget that God is the one that gave Michael Jackson his talent. Regardless of what Hollywood or anyone else says, our culture creates gods of those individuals that are popular and successful, despite their drug habits, sexual impropriety, or other destructive practices or behavior.

Michael Jackson is now gone. He reached the end of his journey. Did he worship God faithfully? Did he acknowledge God for all that He gave him? Did he yield to God and allowed Him to have first place in his life? Did he seek God's help to eliminate his drug problem? Unless the answers to the above questions were "yes," how could he have achieved any happiness in his life?

It is common for people today to respect and honor medical doctors quite a bit more than God. Do not misunderstand me; I think medical doctors are great, especially when you need one. I come from a large extended family, which has produced medical doctors in the past, and currently has a doctor, a dentist, and a nurse practitioner, my sister. However, it is important for the physician to remember that God is the "Great Healer" and all knowledge, ability, and skill comes from Him. I believe that today, modern medicine seems to focus too much on the disease and less on the patient. I would have to conclude that something is certainly lacking spiritually in the treatment or medical care of the patient. Let us remember that God created the human body, and acknowledging Him makes a great deal of sense. Spirituality should be entwined with medicine, since better health outcomes seem to be linked to a higher level of spirituality. Realize that greater results are possible when God is consulted for His intervention. For example, it might be useful for the doctor to give a spiritual questionnaire, like the common physical one that we all complete when we go to see our doctor, which will address spiritual questions, identifying any form of spiritual distress that the patient might be experiencing.

I believe that acknowledging God and the role that He plays in the care of the patient by the physician is monumental in achieving an overall well being of the patient. A good example of this is the 2006 study by Gail Ironson of the University of Miami. She discovered that HIV patients who had become more spiritual since their diagnosis fought off the disease more effectively than their counterparts did. Yes, believing in God can change your health status very significantly. Even more than medication, social, or emotional support, doctors need to become comfortable in discussing the spiritual aspects of a patient's life, since the physical effects related to the patient's spirituality can be so significant in the care of the individual.

Denial of God in the public square is prevalent today as liberalism rises and anything associated with God is rejected. This form of secularism brings about a pluralistic culture, in which the Judeo/Christian faith has been demoted to only one of several alternative faith traditions. Humanism, atheism, agnosticism, and other godless secular belief systems are deemed equal as other viable options in the United States. Therefore, many people consider the Ten Commandments to be just another relic and not appropriate for any governmental entity. Currently, this is what is politically correct in America.

As we look at the phrase, "One Nation under God" we wonder, "Will this also be considered a form of relic"? The United States coins and paper currency bears the motto "In God We Trust." Are these phrases going to be eliminated because society wants to be politically correct? If we eliminate these phrases from our coins and currency, how can we expect God to bless and protect us? The public denial of God, the God of the Bible, makes the statement that, He is no longer considered relevant or appropriate for our culture. This belief is having devastating moral consequences for our nation, self evident in the rise of violent crimes and drug and alcohol abuse.

As we look at God in America today, a Barna Study (www.barna. org), shows that in America 3500 to 4000 churches close their doors each year. Churches lose an estimated 2,765,000 people each year to secularism and nominalism. The proportion of the population that can be classified as Christian declined from 86% in 1990 to 75% in 2009, this last statistic came from a study by the American Religion

Identification Survey. The Barna Study was also clear on the effects of those individuals who do not attend church regularly. It stated that such individuals are more likely to feel stressed out, to be less optimistic, and to believe that they are making a positive difference on the world, and are much less likely to be concerned about the moral condition of the nation. The study also revealed that those who attend church regularly are 35% more likely to live longer.

I have included in this section the "alternative sets of Ten Commandments which many people feel should replace the Judeo-Christian Ten Commandments. The reference that I used to obtain them was "The Society for the Practical Establishment and Perpetuation of the Ten Commandments." They are as follows:

The Humanist Standard Ten Commandments believed to have been written by the Long Island Secular Humanist Society in 1999.

We, the members of the human community speak these words, saying:

1. We shall not limit freedom of thought.
2. We shall not cause unnecessary harm to any living thing or the environment.
3. We shall be respectful of others.
4. We shall be honest.
5. We shall be responsible for our actions.
6. We shall be fair in all matters to all persons.
7. We shall be considerate of the happiness and well-being of others.
8. We shall be reasonable in our actions.
9. We shall nurture these values by word and deed in our children, family, and friends.
10. We shall not limit inquiring or testing by their consequences, or any matter, including these commandments.

Ten Commandments for the Third Millennium:

1. Respect and worship any deity within your faith tradition, if you follow one. Value and support the right of others to do the same.
2. Enjoy and support legal guarantees of freedom of belief, religious freedom, assembly and speech for all.
3. Do not use obscene speech in the name of the deities of any religion. Formally recognized or not.4. Follow the guidance of your faith or secular tradition every day of the week.
5. Help establish social safety nets so that the very young, the elderly, the sick, mentally ill, physically disabled, unemployed, poor and broken will receive adequate medical attention and enjoy at least a minimum standard of living.
6. Minimize the harm you do to others and yourself. Treat others as you wish to be treated.
7. Do not engage in sexual activity with another person, which is coercive, unsafe, manipulative, public, or outside a committed monogamous relationship.
8. Do not steal the property of others except in case of emergency.
9. Do not lie, either in or out of court. Be honest and truthful.
10. Attempt to be satisfied with your current standard of living and do not obsess over the possessions of others.

The Ten Commandments by Lord of Heaven:

Spiritual and Mystical Society:

The Shall Nots:
1. Thou shall not kill.
2. Thou shall not steal.
3. Thou shall not lie.
4. Thou shall not hate.
5. Thou shall not oppress.

The Shalls:
1. Thou shall love.
2. Thou shall create.
3. Thou shall seek knowledge.
4. Thou shall have courage.
5. Thou shall know thyself.

The Native American Ten Commandments:
1. Treat the earth and all that dwell with respect.
2. Remain close to the Great Spirit.
3. Consider the impact on the next six generations when *making decisions.*
4. Work together to benefit all humanity.
5. Freely give help and kindness wherever needed.
6. Do what you believe is right.
7. Look after the well-being of your mind and body.
8. Contribute a share of your efforts to the greater good.
9. Be truthful and honest at all time.
10. Take full responsibility for your actions.

Then there is the Ellory F. Schempp 1963 case which made it to the Supreme Court. Mr. Schempp suggested nine commandments, which are now being followed by many atheists, agnostics, and non-religious worldwide.

1. You are human and neither Jesus, Mohammed, nor Buddha can speak for you. Be courageous and live without a god.
2. Do not injure human beings or animals. But make

Reasonable exceptions.
3. When you see evil, make sure that it is not in a *mirror because sometimes the enemy is us. Emotions are a part of life. Feelings are good. Angry and fearful feelings are valid, but be circumspect.*
4. Morality is about how you treat the life that has been given to you, before you got asked. Once here, try to do some good and leave us a little better than when you arrived. There is no second chance
5. Ideas are good. Some ideas are better than others.
The best way to win is to seek evidence that supports an idea in a way that can be tested and evaluated. Covet not ancient ideas that contradict new evidence.
6. Love one another because love is good. There is no god, nor parent, nor partner that will love you all the time, unconditionally. Keep not fantasies in your minds, but accept reality even when things look dark because there is love around, and all you have to do is tap into it.
7. Sex is good so have fun. Do not hurt another out of Selfishness. Do not worry what sex other might have.
8. Honor your parents, but remember they put their Pants one leg at a time.
9. There is great beauty in the world, on this earth, in music, in the life around us. Take note for it and *you shall be richly rewarded.*

There are many more, but you get the idea. Leave the Judeo/Christian God of the Ten Commandments, completely out, be politically correct, and deny that He ever existed. Then revise, revise, and revise until "you" feel that it expresses what "you" are trying to convey. Then follow these new commandments, which are based on moral relativism, in other words, free to make up your own rules as you see fit. Forget about sin or spiritual death, since it would not be important in today's society, because everything is "relative" to the situation, and there is no accountability to God, certainly not the God of the Bible. Whether it is in the government realm, public realm, or in the private realm, for the many who do not believe in God, or who believe in the gods of other religions, it is fair to say that accountability for sin is non-existent since sin is considered a mistake or a "learning experience" in the life of the soul. A good example of this is the currently televised, adultery confession, by the famous golfer Tiger Woods. He said that he committed the acts of adultery because he felt "entitled" but that he learned from his experiences, and that he is going to return and practice the religion of his family, Buddhism.

The atheists and agnostic group called "Freedom from Religion Foundation" filed a lawsuit with the U.S. District Court seeking to block the engraving of "In God We Trust" and the "Pledge of Allegiance" at the Capital Visitor Center in Washington. The lawsuit states that the motto and the words "Under God" in the Pledge of Allegiance would discriminate against those who do not practice the Judeo/Christian faith. This group is also challenging the constitutionality of the National Day of Prayer in Federal Court. Our nation began as a Judeo/Christian nation, and God blessed it. Slowly over time, our nation's morality has declined to the point that we are aborting babies, just to enjoy a more promiscuous sex life. Many public schools around the nation seem to facilitate pre-married sexual intercourse, through liberal sexual education classes and the passing out of condoms to teenagers. Sex is a natural desire so it's ok; abstinence is not emphasized.

Furthermore, President Obama gave a speech while traveling in Cairo, while in prayer, referring to Moses, Jesus, and Mohammed, the President used the term, "Peace Be upon Them." The term, "Peace be upon them" is used by Muslims to bless the prophets or deceased holy men. According to Islam, Moses, Jesus, and Mohammed are dead prophets. However, for Christians, Jesus is the living and immortal Son of God, the Word made Flesh, God incarnate Christians are still the majority in America, and yet, Mr. President you denied our God, the God of America. In 2007, Senator Obama stated that the God of the Judeo/Christian Bible is not the

God of America. He said that the God of America is diversified, and not necessarily Christian. Recently, President Obama re-stated that the Judeo/Christian God is no longer the God of America. He is willing to hide his faith as a Christian, in order to be "politically correct". He needs our prayers.

My friends, God will not abandon us. Even though we, as a nation are slowly abandoning Him. We have placed "other gods" before Him. We, as a nation, are about to reap the whirlwind of an angry God. Are we going to allow national extremists to lead us down a corrupt path in the name of "freedom" or being "politically correct"? How strong a message does America need from God, in order to stop denying Him publicly? Will we repent and come back to honor the God of the Bible, or do we face destruction of our own doing? There is still time, but is America listening? On the other hand, has America given in to the secularism of the "politically correct" liberal policy?

God wants to change the spiritual nature of humanity. Being like God is ultimately our destiny, but only if we surrender our lives to Him in obedience to His Commandments. America, God said, "I am the Lord your God, who brought you out of your bondage to sin, out of your slavery to Satan. You shall have no other gods before me"! My friends, God is plainly telling us that all of His Laws or commandments are for our own good, and that they serve a very specific purpose and that is that they are to be a blessing and a benefit to humanity. For as humanity develops and establishes a strong personal relationship with the God of Creation, God will provide everything that man needs for his well-being and his survival. It is God's desire that we enjoy and appreciate His gifts to us.

Words to Contemplate:

When I am tempted, and sin against God, His prayer and provision is available.

When I am tested, like Job, His permission is required, and spiritual growth is always acquired.

When I die, like Lazarus, His promise is kept and I am brought to eternal life.

Are you in God's presence today?

Let us pray:

Rouse Your power in Your people, Oh God. With mighty power come and dwell among us. We are in desperate need of Your bountiful grace and mercy. Dear Lord, help us, deliver us, and be our salvation. May You plant in the hearts of every living person the love of Him, Jesus Christ, who is the Way, the Truth, and the Life. Jesus is our refuge and our strength. In the name of Jesus Christ, we pray. Amen.

2

SECOND COMMANDMENT OF GOD

You shall not make for yourself an idol.

"All the people broke off the golden earrings which were in their ears, and brought them to Aaron. And he received the gold from their hand, and he fashioned it with an engraving tool, and made a molded calf. Then they said, "This is your god, O Israel, that brought you out of the land of Egypt"!...And the Lord said to Moses, "Go, get down! For your people whom you brought out of the land of Egypt have corrupted themselves. They have turned aside quickly out of the way which I commanded them. They have made themselves a molded calf, and worshiped it and sacrificed to it, and said, "This is your god, O Israel, that brought you out of the land of Egypt!" And the Lord said to Moses, "I have seen this people, and indeed it is a stiff necked people! Now therefore, let Me alone, that My wrath may burn hot against them and I may consume them"

(Exodus 32:3-4, 7-10).

In the Bible: The Ten Commandments are found in Exodus 20 and Deut.5. In both places, the verses read as follows: "You shall not make for yourself a carved image- any likeness of anything that is in heaven above, or that is in the earth bow down to them nor serve them"

(Exodus 20:4-5).

15

The Second Commandment, as stated in the previous chapter deals with worshipping anything "formed or created by man". A Second Commandment infraction or sin is described as idolatry. When the Prophet Isaiah gave an explanation on what an idol is, he said "it is something men form with their hands". In Isaiah 2:8 we read, "Their land is also full of idols; they worship the work of their own hands, that which their own fingers have made". In the Old Testament, we also read that the Prophet Ezekiel described an idol as something that "men erect in their hearts". It reads as follows: "And the word of YHWH came unto me, saying, Son of Man, these men have set up their idols in their hearts and put the stumbling block of their iniquity before their face" (Ezekiel 14:2-3). Finally, King David was no more charitable with his descriptions concerning idolaters: "Their idols are silver and gold, and the work of men's hands....They that make them are like unto them, so is every one that trusted in them" (Psalm 115:4-8).

As we look at the Second Commandment sins, or transgressions, we need to start with money as being the first false god of modern day society. In the western world of ours, it is simply called "Chasing the Almighty Dollar." People try to compensate for their lack of God, by trying to find satisfaction in money and material things that bring a temporary "high." Such individuals have lifestyles that are devoted completely to the god of money. It is common for these people to sacrifice their values, principles, and relationships for money. It seems that they never have enough, there is something always more to buy or do, and they are never content with what they have. When they feel that they do not have enough of it, then it is the lottery, gambling, or excessive working habits, which will become first in their life. They do these tasks in order to try to make more money. Some people eager for money have sacrificed their families and wandered away from their faith in God. Causing an internal destruction of morals and family values leading to divorce, medically prescribed drug abuse, or alcoholism.

Then there are also the people that work out at the gym five to seven days a week, have perfect eating habits, spend enormous amount of money on vitamins, and special drinks to keep that "perfect body." These people seem to be attracted to other "perfect bodies" and so as the false god of vanity wins, such individuals have created a shrine of their bodies. They spend all their free time working out and so they have no time for church or even prayer. Their idol or god is their perfect body. Therefore, many feel empty and disillusioned with life as ageing or bad health takes away their perfect physique. Remember our bodies will age and die, but our souls are for eternity; nourish them by obeying God's laws.

As I have stated before, many Americans refuse to accept a lack of anything in their lifestyles, they strive to acquire all kinds of merchandise as a means of satisfying a human need to justify their existence. This, of course, is a vain attempt to fill the void that exists in their lives due to the absence of God. However, using material goods to define self-worth is self-destructive as we have seen in this depressed economy, and the foreclosures of "Mac Mansions" across the nation.

Jesus said, "No servant can serve two masters. For either he will hate the one, and love the other, or else he will hold to the one and despise the other. You cannot serve God and money" (Luke 16:13). A person, who worships money or any other form of worldly materialism, can never put God first because his idol will consume him. There will be no time for God, no motivation for God. The god that man creates requires "all" of his time, whether he wants to give it or not.

Then there are those individuals who are not rich, but want to live as though they are and so just about everything that they buy is placed on plastic or credit. Did you ever wonder why the first credit card ever issued in America was called "Master Card"? Think about it, a "master" needs servants or slaves, and how many Americans are enslaved to their credit cards today? These people are sometimes working more than one job, sacrificing time with their families, to be able to make the next credit card payment.

You see my friends; man is prone to invoke his own gods depending on whatever modern practice of idolatry is ruling his life. It could be financial gain, vanity, success, fame, or anything else that pulls him away from the True God of the Universe. The God of the Bible will have no other gods before Him! He is a jealous God.

Christian theologian Paul Tillich, states that, "Idolatry is the elevation of a preliminary concern to intimacy." Tillich's example of modern idolatry is "extreme nationalism". In this case, the state is taken to supreme value while the truth is that it should only hold a "relative" value for the individual. The finite then becomes the infinite in the mind of the individual. You see God is absolute and infinite and only He is worthy of our complete "devotion."

With this commandment, the Lord draws our attention toward Himself as the ultimate Source of our existence and of all goodness in life, as the supreme goal of our existence, and there are no substitutes. The God of the Bible, is the Author of Life, Creator of everything, He is our Father, and merciful Savior. Unfortunately, as I mentioned earlier, in today's modern world, the focus seems to be, for the unbelievers or the Christians alike, great concern for acquiring material wealth, worldly fortunes, having a successful career, obtaining physical gratifications, and attempting to achieve complete happiness. You know, like in many of the movie endings that we see today. Think about all the movie and music stars that are worshipped in today's culture and the political leaders being adored. I can remember when President Obama was on the campaign trail, the news would show women and men actually crying because they were in his presence. Then for others, contemporary science has become the supreme authority by which they judge and, unfortunately, reject the truths revealed by God. You know the rest, drug addiction, drunkenness, smoking, gambling, gluttony, sex, pride, greed, vanity, pride, yes; these have become the masters of many, leading them to the destruction of their souls. See how great is the illusion of this world that blinds so many.

I would like to state that in regards to this commandment, I do not believe that God forbids the honoring of holy icons in churches. For example, in the Roman Catholic Church or the Greek Orthodox Church, Christians do not perceive such icons as deities; instead, they are reminders of spiritual affirmations by God. As God has appeared to Prophets, created angels, became the Savior and Redeemer, and allowed biblical history to show vast amounts of miraculous events, the icons basically, convey what Holy Scripture describes in words. I believe that Christians praying before an icon give honor and glory, not to the icon, but to the One who is depicted by it. You see, man's structure is such that seeing or hearing will greatly influence his thoughts and overall spiritual mood. At this point, it becomes much easier to concentrate on prayer and feel the closeness of God.

It is important to mention that Moses, through whom God forbade the worship of idols, was actually ordered by God to place the gold cherubim on the cover of the Ark of the Covenant. Similarly, God also ordered weaving of the likeness of the cherubim on the curtain separating the Sanctuary from the Holy of Holies and on the inside of the hanging coverings of the tabernacle (Exodus 25:18-22 and 26:1-37). Then in 1 King 6:27-29 and 2 Chronicles 3:7-14, we read that in the temple of Solomon there were sculptures and embroidered likeness of the cherubim, which were approved by God during the dedication of the temple as we read in the Bible: "The glory of the Lord, in the form of a cloud, filled the house of the Lord" (1 Kings 8-11). Many believe that there were no icons of God in the Tabernacle tent or in the temple of Solomon because He had not revealed Himself in the flesh as God Incarnate. However, Jesus Christ sent a miraculous icon of His Face to King Avgar of Edessa. When the king prayed before the icon of Christ, the king was then cured of leprosy. Therefore, I believe that worshipping God or honoring His saints, those that do right in His name, through icons or relics do not contradict the second commandment of God.

Friends, the essence of this commandment is paganism through idolatry. In addition, paganism is a threat, even today, as liberal secularism becomes the god of choice. We sometimes need to be reminded that idolatry, in any form, is strictly forbidden by this commandment, because it will lead to a culture of death. This was true in ancient Babylon and it is true in modern America. Who can deny that today liberal secularism has become the norm, and false gods under the names of "politically correct, choice, or autonomy" are being honored in our society? There must be a conversion of people's hearts to the commandments of the Lord of Life. The "new world view" is leading America away from its founding principles which were divinely grounded in nature. It is important to understand that America is on the brink of eternal perdition, and only God can rescue our land.

America is fighting a battle against Satan. It is called "Spiritual Warfare". Satan is trying to keep us from worshiping the God of the Bible, and from making Him first in everything in our lives. To let something, other than God, get into our heart and take the place of God our Creator, is a grave sin. Satan wants us to worship anything and everything, as long as we do not worship God, the Creator of man.

You see; God is seriously grieved when we are untrue to Him. God is pure Love, and He is wounded when our affections are transferred to anything else. As God hands out punishment for the transgression of this commandment, we should take notice that punishment is visited upon the children unto the "third or the fourth" generation, while mercy is shown unto the "thousand" generation.

This brings to mind a topic that has been discussed in the news media today, "the grandchild tax." The current national debt is called the grandchild tax because we are spending large sums of money that our grandchildren and great grandchildren will have to pay back, thus decreasing their standard of living. This tax burden will bring about a dramatic "shift away" from the foundation of Western civilization. These children will more likely experience higher rates of unemployment, a higher cost of living, higher levels of poverty, and even lack a college education due to the rising cost of tuition and lack of scholarships. Yes, our grandchildren will pay dearly for the "sins of their fathers."

As Western civilization moves away from the Judeo-Christian moral values, God has predicted an incredible turn of events with grave consequences for this nation. As the writers, filmmakers, liberal politicians, and television producers have promoted the "do your own thing morality" and "worship anything and everything" you wish, ranging from famous movie stars, to sports figures, it is not difficult to see the devastating effects that it has had on this country.

It has completely assaulted the moral core of the American people. Even the church establishment seem to have taken "time-off" their responsibilities, as they have downplayed sin and started condoning promiscuity, divorce, and even in some cases, abortion, as liberal churches take a stand for the woman's right to choose an abortion. This is a time, my friends, when Scripture reveals that misguided leaders will call "evil good and good evil" as stated in Isaiah 5:20.

Theologian, Carl Henry described the reemergence in the Western culture of a "pagan mentality" in his book, "The Twilight of a Great Civilization. Mr. Henry believes that "there is no fixed truth, no final good, no ultimate meaning or purpose, and that the living God is a primitive illusion" (The Twilight of a Great Civilization). It also goes on the say that "as the 21st century dawns, American culture is in a mess...the system has lost its moorings, and like ancient Rome is drifting into a dysfunctional situation" (The Twilight of American Culture, pp.1-2). Although he is an atheist, Carl Henry, acknowledges the dysfunction of a culture without "no ultimate meaning or purpose" which is precisely what God offers humanity.

Many view the second commandment as problematic. Some liberal groups say that ".....visiting the iniquity of the fathers upon the children" can raise serious ethical and moral concerns. Because, you see, this implies that innocent descendents will be held responsible for the sins of their parents, grandparents, great- great-grandparents. Evidently, this Commandment seems to "contradict" America's values, the argument out there is "how can you be guilty for something that you did not do"? However, God is severely grieved when we are untrue to Him. Again, God is pure Love, and He is greatly wounded when our affections are transferred to anything but Him. There are consequences for transgressing on this Commandment, and essentially, man will reap what he sows. Whether it is good or bad, children from generations to come will also feel the effect of punishment for this sin.

My friends, there is no room for idolatry of money or greed in those who desire to serve the Lord. Remember the story of the rich young ruler that was told by Jesus to "go and sell all that you have, and give it to the poor, and you shall have treasure in heaven" (Mathew 19:21). Although not everyone is told by God to sell all of their possessions to care for the poor, this was a requirement for the rich young ruler because his great riches had control of his heart. His heart belonged to money and not God. In other words, his god was money.

Another modern day form of idolatry is having a lifestyle of anything that has gotten out of control in your life; usually it is something that is controlling you. This does not only refer to alcohol or drugs. It could also refer to food. There are people who live to eat. In addition, in our culture, it is customary to "super-size" it. In addition, now even small children in America have a problem with obesity. Some might say that obesity is essentially the effect of the "worshipping the god of food."

For many people today, a Second Commandment transgression becomes one of devotion to their work. Workaholics seem to be controlled by their need to work, to earn more money, to buy or pay for more things. These addicts seem to put their health, family, and certainly God behind their busy work schedule, creating a void in their families and one with God. All of the above mentioned, my friends, come from the unseen hands of Satan at work. As the Bible states, "But even if our gospel is veiled, it is veiled to those who are perishing, whose minds of gods of this age has blinded, who do not believe, let the light of the gospel of the glory of Christ, who is the image of God, should shine on them" (2 Corinthians 4:3-4). You see, Satan conditions people to visualize life in this world without God, by "doing it themselves." By blinding most of humanity in this way, Satan has diverted the attention away from God and towards the empty state of material wealth and worldly fortunes.

The Second Commandment is a sure reminder that God is far greater than anything that we can see or imagine. This knowledge must never be pushed aside or replaced by modern day idolatry. We need to know and understand that humanity is destined to become like Him. God wants to permanently change the spiritual nature of humanity, and ultimately transform those who have become like Him in mind and heart, from a physical existence to a spiritual existence and destiny. Remember being like God is our destiny. Nevertheless, we must be in obedience to His commandments. Ultimately, God will hold us accountable for our actions, words, and deeds. Let's face it, we need God in order to restore our lives and collect our eternal inheritance.

Now, take a few moments and reflect on your life. What are your priorities? Is it God and family? What are your goals in life? Is wealth your ultimate goal? What are the passions of your life? What about your intimate relationships with loved ones? What about your relationship with God? Do you even have one?

The second commandment teaches us that "nothing" can be more important in our lives than God. Otherwise, you will always be searching but never finding the peace and love that your soul craves.

We need to be the salt and light that God has called us to be to this world. God did not call us to hide our light under a bushel, instead, lets share God's light and truth with a lost and hurting world. Sadly, when you take God into the world people will not always be nice. However, we are called to be courageous in the face of sin. Rejecting God has been the lifestyle for many in America, and now it is the secular way of our politically correct society. Remember that Jesus told us that the harvest would be plentiful but the laborers would be few. So, do not be discouraged and keep God's message alive. Go proudly and proclaim the Gospel of the Lord and He shall bless you freely.

Words to Contemplate:
The Twelve promises of God to the Christian to claim:

1. *God's Presence: "I will never leave you" (Heb.13:5).*
2. *God's Protection: "I am your shield" (Gen.15:1).*
3. *God's Power: "I will strengthen you" (Isa.41:10).*
4. *God's Provision: "I will help you" (Isa.41:10).*
5. *God's Leads: "And when He puts forth His own sheep, He goes before them"(John 10:4).*
6. *God's Purposes: "I know the thoughts that I think towards you,*

says the Lord, and they are thoughts of peace and not evil" (Jer. 20:11).

7. God's rest: "Come unto me, all ye that labor and are heavy laden, and I will give you rest" (Matt.11:28).

8. God's Cleansing: "If we confess our sins, He is faithful and just to forgive us our sins, to cleanse us from all unrighteousness" (1 John 1:9).

9. God's Goodness: "No good thing will He withhold from them that work uprightly" (Ps.84:11).

10. God's Faithfulness: "The Lord will not forsake His people for His great name's sake" (1Samuel 12:22).

11. God's Guidance: "The meek He will guide.]" (Ps.25:9).

12. God's Plan: "All things work together for the good, to those that love God" (Rom.8:28).

Let us pray:

Oh Mighty and Merciful God. You are our strength in body, our courage in spirit, and our patience in sorrow and pain. Dear Lord, accept our sincere prayer, because without You, we are weak and can do nothing good. Kindly give us the greatest gift of all, Your grace. So that we may keep your commandments and always please You in thought, word, and deed. In Jesus Christ, we pray. Amen.

3

THIRD COMMANDMENT OF GOD

You shall not take the name of the Lord, your God in vain, for the Lord will not hold him guiltless who takes his name in vain.
(Exodus 20:7).

Lord, help me to always use Your Name with honor and respect. May I be under the awe of Your power, and use Your most holy name in reverence and admiration. Father, we know that the time has come for Your children to defend You against the blasphemer and to defend Your laws against the unrighteous and the unbeliever. Father give us courage and we will go with a zeal in our hearts and carry Your banner of love eternally. For only You are worthy of worship. In Jesus Christ, we pray. Amen.

On July 25, 2009, the *Washington Examiner* wrote an article, titled, "Will Biden apologizes for using Christ's name as a curse word." To date, no he has not, and probably will not. So why isn't there uproar of complaints? Because sadly many people use the name of the Christian God, Jesus Christ, as a curse word, and the secular society has become desensitized to its highly offensive nature. People are using God's name in empty, worthless, and insignificant ways. This of course, being very offensive to the billions of Christians who accept Jesus as Creator and God of the universe. Joe Biden, who identifies himself as a Christian, and is currently our Vice President, is certainly not setting a good example for the rest of the nation or the world for that matter. Can you imagine what would happen if "Allah" was used in the same manner that some people use the name of our Lord, Jesus Christ? You see, the use of Jesus Christ as a course word is comparable to taking the name of "Allah" in vain. Both mean "God" and it is a breachment of the Ten Commandments either way.

In the 19th century, there was a famous philosopher named Friedrich Nietzsche, and he wrote some essays about the death of God in self and in society. Nietzsche predicted that one day God would become meaningless in general and people would disregard God's influence in society. More and more we are seeing this in all areas of our public life. Blasphemy and ultimate lack of respect for God is becoming not just more apparent, but actually in style. People are angry with God and they clearly state it in all forms of entertainment venues, especially music.

Here in America many people not only use God's name in vain, but they hear it in their music and on the "big screen" and it is completely acceptable by the population in general. God's last name is not DAMN, although it seems to be what He is called in movies and rap videos and songs. Cable TV and even late night regular TV commonly ridicules all forms of spiritual matters. If you ever turn on the TV to the Conan O'Brian show, you might witness blasphemes of the Lord, Jesus Christ. Late night cartoons and MTV videos seem to use the name of the Lord in vain as their insignia under the freedom of speech act.

The Third Commandment essentially forbids the irreverent and disrespectful use of the name of God. Examples would be in jokes, meaningless conversations, swearing in the name of God (habitual oaths in casual conversation), blasphemy, sacrilege (when people make fun of sacred things), and breaking promises made to God.

So what difference does it make whether or not we take the Lord's name in vain? It makes a lot of difference! For one thing, it speaks to the tone of our society and the lack of respect that it has for God. The name of God designates Him as the Supreme and Almighty Creator, and with His name comes miraculous power. For example, think of all the people in the Bible who invoked God's name with faith and in reverence; and instantly, the natural world submitted to God's will. Remember, Moses divided the waters of the Red Sea by invoking the name of God. In addition, in the New Testament, there have been many miraculous healings and the exorcism of evil spirits by the invocation of the name of the Son of God, Jesus Christ. Yet, using profanity to disrespect God has become part of everyday speech for many. Thus, using God in vain is a casual form of speech and most claim that they do not even realize what they are doing. As a culture, we have become desensitized to such language relating to the God of the universe.

When God said in Exodus 20:7, "You shall not take the name of the Lord your God in vain," He was saying that His name is Holy and cannot be used lightly or for no reason. When we commit a transgression of the third Commandment, we are misusing God's name, and although it has become a habit in our society, I cannot help but think of Friedrich Nietzsche's prediction of a society with a meaningless God. When God is ridiculed and mocked, He becomes meaningless to the people in that culture. What does this mean? It means that our culture will exhibit clear signs of decay and ultimately, death. Whether it is a higher crime rate, abortions, or euthanasia, life will hold no value and will disintegrate in front of our very eyes. America cannot continue to allow the media to disregard and disrespect this commandment of God. The people of God must speak up and protect God's basic truth, which is that of the Ten Commandments.

God is not to be taken nonchalantly by anyone at anytime. Jesus said, "I say to you, every sin and blasphemy will be forgiven men, but the blasphemy against the Spirit will not be forgiven ... I say to you that for every idle word men may speak, they will give account of it in the day of judgment. For by your words you will be justified and by your words you will be condemned" (Mathew 12:31,36-37).

You see, to dishonor God's name in any way is to denigrate His holiness. It is a way of saying that God is worthless or even non-existent and there is simply no accountability.

Unfortunately, in the past I have been guilty of misusing God's name. When shocked or amazed I have used the occasional, "Oh my G-d." However, I called upon the Lord to help me cease from using such a phrase. Almost immediately, I became overly aware of my usage of the word God inappropriately, and I stopped misusing His name completely. God will assist the soul that invites His help in clearing away sinful behavior immediately.

Today it is common practice to swear under oath in courtrooms around the nation. The problem comes about when the people, who took the oath to tell the truth in the name of God, proceed to lie. Not only is this perjury, but it is a transgression, a sin, or a violation of the third commandment. In the Old Testament, God says, "You shall not swear by my name falsely, and so profane the name of your God: I am the Lord" (lev.19:12).

Remember the late President Nixon and the Watergate tapes; he swore under oath that he was not involved in the Watergate incident. We now know that his statement was not true, to say the least. In addition, if you ever get a chance, or even want to listen to the Watergate tapes, which have since been transcribed, you will see that they were full of blasphemy and profanity. The third commandment was certainly breached, and it is clear to see how sin destroyed the life and career of a President of the United States of America.

Then in 1998, the news broke that a twenty-two year old White House intern by the name of Monica Lewinsky has made allegations of sexual contact with then President Clinton. However, on January 26, 1998, President Clinton with his wife, Hilary Clinton, spoke at a White House press conference and issued a forceful denial, "I did not have sexual relations with that woman." In addition, Hilary Clinton stood by her husband throughout the ordeal. In an appearance on NBC's Today Show she said, "The great story here for anybody willing to find it, write about it and explain it is the vast right wing conspiracy that has been conspiring against my husband since the day he announced for president." Even in sworn depositions, President Clinton denied having any "sexual relations" with Monica Lewinsky. Ultimately, when proof was provided, President Clinton was held in contempt of court, his license to practice law was suspended in Arkansas and later by the United States Supreme Court, and he was fined $90,000 for giving false testimony.

During the Clinton scandal, much like during the Tiger Woods scandal, many alleged that the matter was private, and in the case of President Clinton, that sometimes one has to lie, even under oath to protect a very valuable reputation. However, I think that if he told the truth from the beginning, the history books would have been much kinder to him. For it would have showed President Clinton as a man of integrity and commitment to God. Even under difficult situations, he persevered in God.

Breaking the third commandment by invoking the name of Jesus Christ brings to mind a New Testament Bible story. It is the story of the seven sons of Sceva, whom the Apostle Paul met on his first mission to Ephesus. The Apostle Paul had an amazing visit while he was in Ephesus. There Paul performed many miracles, including baptizing many in the name of Jesus Christ, all receiving many blessings including the Holy Spirit. Everything that Paul did, he did in the name of Jesus Christ, and he always got the result he wanted, whether it was healings or exorcisms. However, while Paul was doing his ministry, there were a group of men watching, and they noticed that by Paul invoking the name of Jesus Christ, astonishing things would happen. Evidently, there was something very special about this name. Therefore, they thought they would try it for themselves. Well, read it for yourself and see what happened next:

"Then some of the itinerant Jewish exorcists undertook to invoke the name of the Lord Jesus over those who had evil spirits, saying, "I adjure you by the Jesus, whom Paul proclaims." "Seven sons of a Jewish high priest named Sceva were doing this. But the evil spirit answered them, "Jesus I know, and Paul I recognize, but who are you?" And the man in whom was the evil spirit leaped on them, mastered all of them and overpowered them, so that they fled out of that house naked and wounded (Acts 19:13-16).

The moral of the story is that the seven sons of Sceva misused God's name. They used God's name for their own personal gain, for their own advantage. They dishonored God by manipulating Him in speech and deed. In addition, they received a beating from the evil spirit, consequently, for their actions. The truth is that there are consequences for transgression against the third commandment. Remember God is serious about usage of His name. It deals with

29

His reputation as our Creator and Giver of Life. We have laws against slander. God's laws are His Commandments. If you take the name of God in vain, you will be punished. That is the bottom line, according to the Judeo/Christian Bible, it is a violation of the third commandment.

Here are some examples of miss-using God's name: God's name is misused when we profess God's name but do not mean it; when we use it in a cursing manner; when we pray to Him but do not believe in Him due to lack of faith; when we swear in God's name falsely, when we speak evil of God; when things don't turn out the way you planned; when God is mocked; and in any way using profane or abuse of His Word.

Friends, there is hope. God will forgive anyone who sincerely repents of the sin and asks for forgiveness. Furthermore, God will not only forgive, but He will also help you reform your habits so that you will not commit this sin again. God will place His words of glory and praise on your lips for the honor of His name.

Currently, we are living in very difficult times. God is essentially being expelled and denied in just about every facet of the public life in America today. As children of God, we need to proclaim His name and uphold His Commandments. We are required to speak out as God's people in order to lift His name to glory. We must put ourselves in the line with others to honor God, so that He will continue to prevail in the American way of life.

While America was founded on the God of Creation, Man now denies this evident "Truth." The Laws of this "Truth" are the Ten Commandments. Make no mistake about it, today's secular society has a goal, and that goal is to demolish the Judeo/Christian values that this country was created on. Let's face it, when you can't pray using the name of the Lord in public because it's against the law of man, or because it is not politically correct, or abortion is not called murder, then as Isaiah 5:20 states, "Then evil is now called good and darkness is now called the light."

It is interesting to state that while our laws of "truth" were founded on the God of Creation, it seems that man now, through law, denies this inherent "Truth" and calls it separation of church and state. I believe that this is so because man feels that he is in full control of his life and his destiny. However, the only self-evident truth is that we need to return to the Commandments of God as a nation. Only then will we acquire the blessings of God as 'One Nation under God' again.

Words to Contemplate:

1. *We are God's people and we have been chosen by God to be a part of His Kingdom. To be chosen by God means to be given the opportunity to identify with God.*

2. *We are being sanctified daily. This simply means that God has a specific purpose for each one of us in our lives.*

3. *We have been guaranteed eternal life in heaven. How? Hear the Word of God and accept it as true. Respond in obedience by repenting of sin and following the Ten Commandments, confessing belief in Christ and being baptized into Him.*

4. *Once this has been done, your hope will not perish, spoil, or fade.*

5. *This hope is given freely to anyone who is willing to place their trust in the sacrifice that Jesus Christ made on the cross.*

Let us pray:

Holy God, come among us, Your people, and deliver us from sin. You have given us Jesus Christ, Your only Begotten Son, to take our nature upon Himself, to be crucified and to die for our salvation. Dear God, sow in the hearts of men a true love for Him, our Redeemer. Give us the confidence and the courage to stand up for what is right and just. May the honor and glory be His now and forever. Amen.

4

FOURTH COMMANDMENT OF GOD

Remember the Sabbath day and keep it holy.

Six days you shall labor and do all thy work, but the seventh day is the Sabbath of the Lord thy God: In it you shall not do any work, you, nor your son, nor your daughter, your manservant, nor your maidservant, nor your cattle, nor the stranger that is within your gates: for in six days the Lord made heaven and earth, the sea, and all that is in them, and rested in the seventh day: wherefore the Lord blessed the Sabbath day and hallowed it"

(Exodus 20:8-11).

"In those days, I saw people in Judah treading winepresses on the Sabbath, and bringing in sheaves and loading donkeys with wine, grapes, figs, and all kinds of burdens, which they brought into Jerusalem on the Sabbath day. And I warned them about the day on which they were selling provisions. Men of Tyre dwelt there also, who brought in fish and all kinds of goods, and sold them on the Sabbath to the children of Judah and in Jerusalem.

Then I contended with the nobles of Judah, and said to them, "What evil thing is this that you do, by which you profane the

32

Sabbath day"? Did not your fathers do thus, and did not our God bring all this disaster on us and on this city? Yet you bring added wrath on Israel by profaning the Sabbath."

So it was, as the gates of Jerusalem, as it began to be dark before the Sabbath, that I commanded the gates to be shut, and charged that they must not be opened until after the Sabbath. Then I posted some of my servants at the gates, so that no burdens would be brought in on the Sabbath Day (Nehemiah 13:15-19).

Passages of Scripture from the New Testament such as Acts 20-7, Colossians 2:16-17, Corinthians 16:2 and Revelation 1:10 indicate that Christians are to observe the Sabbath on the Lord's Day, which is Sunday instead of Saturday. Saturday is the day of the Jewish Sabbath.

Here we are in the 21st century and we are always rushed and never seem to have enough time for leisure. It is an age of labor saving devices, with computers in almost every household in the nation, blackberries in our pocket and purses, cell phones; all letting us know when the next meeting is going to take place, and where we have to be, hour by hour, day by day. Yet our work is never completed, and as a nation, we have never been busier. Many complain that there does not seem to be enough time to do all the things that need to be done in a day, especially those things that one considers being important. It is a fact that as we become more advanced in the field of technology, which is supposed to be saving us time and effort. However, people are spending less and less time with their spouses, their children, their community, and their God. There is never enough time to do it all!

For some, keeping the Sabbath holy, as a day of worship, a day for rest, and a day for peace seems to be almost impossible because society feels that it is not being productive. When billionaire Bill Gates was questioned why he did not believe in God, he said, "Just in terms of allocation of time resources, religion is not very efficient. There's a lot more that I could be doing on a Sunday morning."

As the raging waves of materialism increases, man strives for greater things. It is not only owning a home, it is a larger and nicer home in a better neighborhood, and of course, fashionable furniture for every room of the house; it is not just owning a car for transportation, it is a newer car, maybe the latest model available. In addition, since we are working harder and longer hours to pay for it all, we feel that we deserve it, that we are entitled to it, but there will be no time for families, friends, prayer, or God.

In recent decades, as technology advances, the pace of life has accelerated dramatically, and many now experience daily situations that require continuous action and no rest. Being "on call" almost 24/7. Since there is no time for rest and relaxation, as a society, we are eliminating sound practices that in the past have provided much rest to a tired nation. Sunday used to be a day dedicated to the issues of the soul. Going to church, prayer, Scripture reading, meditation on spiritual matters, enlightenment of the mind and spirit, spiritual or religious discussions, and offering acts of mercy to the community at large. For example, visiting the homebound, nursing homes, hospitals, or prisons were all good activities to properly dedicate the day to God. However, times have changed.

I can't even remember the number of people that I have counseled in the last decade or so, which were experiencing incapacitating daily stress, so much that it was affecting them physically, some even coming down with cancer. High blood pressure, leading to heart attacks and strokes, unfortunately, has become too common of a problem in modern America. While others experience symptoms of anxiety and depression, they take medication, but find no relaxation, so they take more medication. Unfortunately, until they come to terms with their life, they will receive no internal rest. As I look back, I can remember quite a few people, who did not regain their lives back from the excess responsibilities of this modern world, and ultimately they snapped. Heart attacks at 35,severe anxiety attacks at 25, cancer and diabetes due to our fast food diets at 40, depression and suicide at 36, and there are those who are a walking time bomb, ready to explode under the least amount of pressure. There are also many broken relationships and divorces, which have become a common trait of our society, affecting more children every day. Then there are those that due to their stressful life they have become hooked into an un-healthy life style where smoking, drinking, and taking sleep aids have become their way of life. The problem that started as an emotional issue quickly becomes a physical one, and next comes the headaches, migraines, muscular aches and pains, teeth grinding, insomnia, and a decrease in energy levels. Is in it time to take your life back? All you have to do is to comply with what God has already commanded of you. God commands us all to "rest."

The fourth commandment is giving us explicit instructions on how to keep the Sabbath day holy. God commanded us to devote weekly, a complete day to Him. Then in remembrance of the Sabbath, He wanted to sanctify this day, and God wanted this day to be sacred. The Lord wanted the Sabbath to be used for rest and for worship. He wanted us to take care of ourselves, physically, emotionally, and spiritually. God said, "Six days you shall labor, and do all your work but the seventh day is a Sabbath to the Lord your God" (Exodus 20:9).

They were known by a variety of names, Sunday blue laws, closing laws, Sunday regulations, and Sunday statues. The blue laws, from their inception, regulated a series of activities in our nation on Sundays, which ranged from buying liquor, buying cigarettes, to buying a house or a car. The intent of this law was to keep the Sabbath day holy. Closing business or banning certain activities on Sundays assured that the Sabbath, would be respected and it would truly be a day of rest. Activities such as hunting or drinking alcohol would be prohibited under the blue laws.

Blue laws have a long history with our nation dating back to Colonial times in the New Haven colonies around the late 17th century. These laws were initially formed by the Puritan colonies in the "New World," and, interestingly enough, were printed on blue paper. These laws mostly came from Christian mainstream America that focused on enforcing the moral code of the Ten Commandments. However, if you were Jewish, then there would be some slight difference to the law. The law would be active on Saturday for Shabbat, the Jewish Sabbath, instead of Sunday.

Everything changed in 1961 when the Supreme Court issued four rulings that rejected such laws. The rulings were based on the equal protection clause of the 14th Amendment and the religious liberty clauses of the First Amendment of our Constitution. The argument was that these laws violated the free exercise clause of the First Amendment by imposing a disadvantage on those individuals whose Sabbath day was not on Sunday. It was also felt that the laws violated the establishment clause by endorsing one religion over another, favoring Christianity.

The most famous rulings on the blue laws came from the McGowan case and the Braunfeld case. The McGowan case arose after several Maryland department store employees were charged and convicted for selling store items on a Sunday. In the state of Maryland only bread, milk, gas and a few other necessary items could be sold on Sundays. In the Braunfeld case, Orthodox Jews sued in federal court stating that the blue laws violated their constitutional rights. The time had come in America to re-evaluate the constitutionally of the blue laws. Slowly but surely, the ban on Sunday's sales of alcohol and other non-essential items were removed from most states.

America's blue laws were designed to enforce moral and religious standards, particularly the observance of Sunday as a day of worship and rest. Christmas Day, Thanksgiving, and Easter were considered days of religious observance and thus, validating the closing of many secular establishments, including the outlawing of the sale of alcohol. Today most of these laws have been repealed, being declared unconstitutional, and are not enforced. In many states, blue laws have been retained as a matter of tradition. It is interesting to note that laws of this type are also found in non-Christian cultures such as Israel, where the day concerned is Saturday rather than Sunday, and Saudi Arabia where the month of Ramadan is involved and a time for many secular store closings.

As the economy places most states in the worst fiscal shape in recent history, relaxation of the nation's moral code is unfortunately, a given. Lifting regulations on Sunday alcohol sales with the aim of raising tax revenues is one way that many states are dealing with their deficits. Therefore, what we are looking at is another lost battle between commercialization and God. Some have even gone as far to say that consumerism is actually a new form of idolatry. We have lost the sacredness of the Sabbath as shopping becomes "compressed" into the weekend. This "now open Sundays" is just another battle lost between church and state proving just how secular America has become. God does not play a central role in daily life for the American community anymore. Sabbath keeping and secularism mix about as well as oil and water.

It is vital to understand that the Sabbath "rest" comes from God. God gave us this day of rest as a gift of grace. This is the day when He can give us peace of mind, restore our energy, refresh us with renewed strength, and eases our anxious mind, as we communicate with Him in prayer. "The Sabbath was made for man" (Mark 2:27). Is there anything that we need more than rest? Everywhere, there is unrest today. There is unrest in society, in the church, in the family, and in the soul of men. The Fourth Commandment requires God's people to cease from their ordinary work and rest. Come to God and rest. This is a day that has been consecrated unto God, and God has given much grace to it.

I think that Jesus said it best, regarding this commandment to the visionary in Georgia, Nancy Fowler. "Everything needs to be in balance in order for it to work properly. If one wheel in a machine is broken, it will affect the entire machine. By My helping you stay in balance, I am helping you come back to Me. Your journey in life is a journey back to God, back to me." "Each one of My commandments is an aid, is a step, to help you love Me and one another. Do not treat My commandments as thou shall not do this or that, but that thou shall love more. All commandments are an aid to help you grow in love. As plants and trees grow, as an infant grows, so is it destined for all humans to grow in love. Look at it this way. Every human being is given a tiny seed of My perfect Love. This seed is destined to grow in the fullness of My Love. You can't keep the Sabbath holy unless you examine and improve yourself and make amends for the sins committed during the previous six days. Take time to reflect upon My goodness and My Love" (ourlovingmother.org/ten commandments). Jesus said it brilliantly; the Sabbath day should be a day of reflection and prayer, in dedication to God. It is the day to replenish the soul.

What about those people who have to work on Sunday, such as doctors and nurses? According to the Bible, we are supposed to abstain from secular work on the Sabbath, with three exceptions.

1. Works of Mercy. This includes doctors, nurses, paramedics, firefighters, and even general hospital staff such as emergency room personnel.
2. Works of Necessity. A good example is eating. This would include restaurants and cafeterias.
3. Works directly related to God and His kingdom. That would be the minister, pastor, priest, rabbi, religion teachers, or other personnel in your place of worship.

With all the trials and tribulations that our society faces today, as it staggers on the brink of moral collapse, it becomes imperative to observe the Sabbath and to keep it holy.

Those of us who remember the days of the "blue laws," when alcohol was not sold on Sundays, stores closed, and most services had reduced hours, it was a time when the Lord was the top priority in American life. Family was important next to God, houses could be left unlocked, Sunday night family meals included everyone at the table, and the family would watch television shows together suitable for the whole family. Shows like the "*Wonderful World of Disney*" were a family treat in most American households. However, now on regular TV, prime time Sundays offer families shows such as *Desperate Housewives* and *Sex in the City*. How can we possibly withstand the pressures and problems of worldliness unless we are grounded in the divine will of God?

In conclusion, the Sabbath is a reminder of our Creator, who not only created the universe, but also His Spirit-filled people and His wonderful purpose for humanity. God is honored when the Sabbath is celebrated and kept holy. It is a day to put away the to-do list, to stop shopping or buying, and to quit worrying about the profit margin. In a culture that treats Sunday like any other day of the week, and manages to turn all that is sacred into something secular, we need to resist the tendency to allow our work to enslave us into the grave.

I believe that the problem with our society is that most people find it hard to take a genuine delight in the sanctified pleasures of

God. You see, God is calling us away from our own personal affairs in life, and is calling us to participate in the most important affair of all, the glorification, and worshiping of our Lord. When we place our personal pleasures first, then we miss the greatest pleasure of all, fellowship with the One and Only Living God. Keeping the fourth commandment does offer the Christian freedom. Yes, you can go to a restaurant, and take your dogs to the park. God is not a tyrant; He is a loving and caring God. So, take my advice, live life for God, enjoy the Sabbath, and listen to the God of Creation Who is probably lovingly saying, "Take a break my child, come to me, for I, your God, will give you rest."

My friends remember that America was established on the worship of the One True God. And yet, as more Americans have abandon the Judeo/Christian faith with the different religions and beliefs of our time, unfortunately, dedicating the Sabbath to the Lord, has been one of the first commandments to go. So, let us not forget God, and give thanks and praise to the God that preserved us in peace and strengthened us in adversity. May He graciously keep us in the "Palm of His hand".

Words to Contemplate:

A man whispered, "God, speak to me."
And a meadowlark sang. But the man did not hear.
So the man yelled, "God, speak to me!"
And thunder rolled across the sky. But the man did not listen.
The man looked around and said, "God let me see you." A star shone brightly. But the man did not notice it.
The man shouted, "God, show me a miracle." And a baby was born but the man was unaware.
So, the man cried in despair, "Touch me God, and let me know that you are here!" Whereupon God reached, down and touched the man. But the man brushed the butterfly away from his cheeks and walked away.
Moral: Don't miss the blessing because it's packaging is not what you might expect. Source Unknown.

Let us pray:

Almighty and everlasting God. Give unto us the grace to stop and take a respite on the Sabbath. Allow this day to be sacred as we follow the path of holiness. Allow us to accept Your gift of rest. Father, we bless You for Your Creation, preservation, and for Your abounding love towards us. Lord, help us to realize what is important in this fleeting life. Protect us against worldly anxieties and faithless fears and give us Your eternal peace. In Christ, we pray. Amen.

5

FIFTH COMMANDMENT OF GOD

Honor your father and your mother, that your days may be long upon the land which the Lord your God is giving you.

(Exodus 20:12)

Moses said, "Honor your father and mother," and he who curses his father and mother, let him be put to death." But I say, "If a man says to his father or mother, "Whatever profit you might have received from me is Corban"(gift of God), then you no longer let him do anything for his father or his mother, making the word of God of no effect through your tradition which you have handed down. And many such things you do"

(Mark 7: 10-12).

The Fifth Commandment of God introduces man to a series of commandments that define proper relationships with his fellow man. The fifth commandment through the tenth commandment essentially deals with the acceptable standard of conduct in human behavior, as stated by God. It is usually said that the first four commandments explain how to establish a relationship with the God of Creation, while the last six commandments explain how to

41

establish a relationship with other human beings. In as much as we owe our birth to our parents, the fifth commandment specifically instructs us to "obey our parents in all things". If we obey this commandment, then there are rewards promised by God for those who honor their parents. For the Lord says that for those that honor their parents, "their days may be long upon the land which the Lord your God is giving you". This commandment promises prosperity and longevity to those that comply with this commandment.

Unfortunately, today there are many forces at work in our society to encourage the nature of rebellion in our children, and at times, making it acceptable to question the authority of their parents. If children are not taught while they are young to honor and respect their parents, they certainly will not do it when they become adults. Western society emphasizes and rewards individualism in young adults. Therefore, decision making in youths, without regards to parental counseling is common today. Self-expression, no matter how radical, sometimes becomes the norm in certain areas of the country. Children with black finger nail polish, black lipstick, and body piercing are telling their parents that they are too old fashioned, and that they (kids) are misunderstood. Our culture says that it is healthy for young adults to have some form of self-expression. Yet, it is sometimes difficult for parents to discern how much of this rebelliousness to allow as an expression of growing and healthy independence.

On the other hand, adolescents who are becoming aware of the imperfections and shortcomings of their parents seem to be confused by the messages that our secular society is sending them. Our society openly declares that the personal faults of the parent negate all of their parental authority. This gives the children almost an "ok" for disrespecting their parents, without teaching them the appropriate way of communicating their feelings within a family unit. Children without such tools become crippled by stored anger and resentment towards their parents. Past arguments or disagreements become magnified in the child's memory, making healing a very slow and painful process for the entire family.

How, then do we understand the meaning of "honor your father and mother"? I think that first it should be mentioned that the Lord did not say, "Honor only model fathers and mothers." The fact is that we are all human and we all make mistakes, but it is a greater mistake to judge parents by a personal standard or the standards of the world. It is better to allow God to deal with them, personally, on judgment day. Remember that in the Lord's Prayer, Jesus instructs us to "Forgive us our trespasses as we forgive those who trespass against us." My advice for the child is, honor your parents by forgiving them. You cannot continue to blame them for how they raised you, because parenting does not come naturally to everyone. Ultimately, the Bible teaches us that if we do not forgive those that have hurt us, then God, will not forgive us when we ask Him for forgiveness. It is important to forgive because it allows the soul to heal. Remember, God allows us to repent and come back to Him at anytime, anywhere, and under any circumstances.

A good example of this is that of King David. King David committed adultery and then had his lover's husband, Uriah, murdered while he successfully schemed to covet Uriah's beautiful wife called Bathsheba. Nevertheless, our God, the God of Creation and Compassion, still chose him to be the earthly ancestor of Jesus Christ. In fact, the Jewish race, up to this very day, reveres him as their most illustrious king. What an amazing God we serve!

I think that another way in which parents are honored is when someone gives you a compliment on how well you treat others, raised your children, serve God, or serve your society. Has anyone given you such a compliment? If they have, then be sure that your parents played a significant role in raising such a good human being.

Unfortunately, there are those people who spend their whole life living in bitterness, anger, and resentment because they feel their parents either did not show enough love or praise, or maybe because they were disciplined too much, or weren't given enough attention. Well, it is time to stop complaining, to be responsible, and to grow up and forgive your parents. Furthermore, thank them for the great job that they did raising you. Put the past behind you and let God heal and take care of the rest.

As a Hospice Chaplain, I routinely visited patients living in nursing homes. After so many years of making visits, I came away with the indication that nursing homes can be either a blessing or a curse. They can be a blessing for those people who have no one to take care of them, and, the staff and other residents become their family. However, they can be a curse for those patients who have family members in large enough homes, but refuse to take care of them. Therefore, they live the rest of their days feeling rejected by their loved ones. When I was young, I remember growing up in a household with my parents and maternal grandparents. Even when they became extremely ill, we would have a CNA come to the home, for a couple of hours a day to help take care of them. The rest of the time, family members would take turn caring for them. Some of my most memorable moments as a child were my long conversations with my grandfather, in our back patio, eating oranges from our trees. Interestingly, the conversations were not as important as the time spent sharing an orange from our orange trees. One way to honor your parents is to take care of them when they can no longer take care of themselves. Unfortunately, western society has moved away from this concept, and I believe that it ultimately does the family unit quite a disservice. So many memories will not be created, and many valuable relationships will not have had a chance to be formed. Traditions will pass away unnoticed, as grandparents and parents die.

Does this commandment apply to the grownups? The answer to this is yes! If you are employed, do you obey your employer and honor your boss? Do you do it because if you do not you might be fired or do you do it because it pleases God? In addition, for those of you that work at home, do you take care of your responsibilities? Do you take care of the children, help them with their homework, and prepare meals for your family? Even if those meals are simple and require little time to prepare. By doing this, you are not just honoring your spouse, but you are also honoring and pleasing God. You see, the choices we make in life, even our mistakes, can ultimately bring honor and glory to God, if we grow in love with God and each other. God can take any situation and turn it into good.

On Feb. 22, 1991, Jesus again appeared to the visionary in

Georgia and her journal states, "My dearest daughter, let me teach you about this commandment of God....Earthly parents are called to imitate us, to be our hands, feet, and heart. You are not to judge the shortcomings of your father and mother. Parents, you are not to judge the shortcomings of your children. Both of you are called to love as we love you. Grow more in love with God and with each other." "I tell you, if you are hurt by your parents or if you, parents, are hurt by your children, respond as I do when you hurt Me... In Love. Never stop loving. My love is unconditional for you. I say again, imitate us, dear children. My children are everyone, the unborn, born, young, old, lame, healthy, poor, wealthy, prideful, and the humble." "No one is not My child, even though you may choose to disown Me. I am the Creator and you are My created children. I call you, all of you, unto Me. I will never abandon you. Please, do not abandon Me. If you abandon this commandment, you abandon Me. What you do to the least of My brothers, you do unto Me". Therefore, it is important that parents and children honor each other always." (End of quote by Jesus.)

In His sermons, the Lord, Jesus Christ reminded the Jewish people of the importance of honoring one's parents (Mark 7:10). Jesus being the Son of God respected his earthly parents. Jesus submitted to His mother, Mary, and would help Joseph in his daily work as a carpenter. In addition, Mathew 15:4-6, Jesus reproaches the Pharisees who under the guise of dedicating their wealth to God refused needful support to their parents. Again, Jesus is teaching us that as a Christian, we must show respect to every person, in accordance with age and status in life.

This commandment reveals that children are beneficiaries of three rewards for those who honor their parents. The rewards are as follows: The first reward for those who honor their parents is grace and glory. That is grace for the current life and glory for the eternal life to come. The second reward is that of a long life. God promises a long and full life to those who show reverence to their parents. The third reward for those who honor their parents, is to have in turn, children who are grateful, pleased, and full of honor for them.

Let me state here that there is one time, when in fact, we

must "disobey" authority according to God. That is when those in authority, our parents or superiors, demand of us something contrary to the Law of God. Then we must say to them what the Apostles said to the Jewish Rabbis when they insisted that the Apostles should not preach about Jesus Christ: "We ought to obey God rather than men" (Acts 4:19, 5:29). Also, remember that when there is conflict between obeying the Divine or men, the Divine must always be obeyed. At this point one should be ready to endure whatever the outcome might be for completely obeying God. In the Christian faith, suffering is at times an integral part of our Christian calling, and will be greatly rewarded in heaven by Him, Who suffered greatly from the hands of unjust rulers (Matt. 5:11-12).

It is also important to state that children need constant encouragement and frequent acknowledgement for their accomplishments and achievements. Most of all they need love and praise if they are going to develop into strong and confident human beings. Remember, our Lord intends for the family to be the first school, the first hospital, the first government, and the first church that our children will experience. Furthermore, such experiences will determine your children's outlook towards life, and the type of relationship that they will ultimately have with God. Like the old saying goes, "charity does begin at home."

Interviews with psychologists, teachers, and parents indicate that of all the factors, which influence our youth, none dominates them more than television. American children watch an average of three to four hours of TV per day and on weekends even more. Therefore, TV is a powerful influence on the development of a child's behavior. The events they witness daily on TV become an acceptable way of behavior. Since most of the shows on TV tend to be violent, children have become immune to the horror of violence in our culture. They gradually accept violence as a way to resolve problems and ultimately, they imitate the violence that they observe on TV. Essentially, these children, teens, or young adults begin to identify with the characters on the shows that they are watching, and those characters become the one's honored and respected. Parents seem to have become the "bad guys" if they practice biblical rules and more often than not, considered too "strict" for today's society, and certainly not in line with what are being shown on TV.

God understands that if a child dishonors his parents, the child will ultimately also dishonor Him. Therefore, the family unit is of extreme importance when referring to this commandment. However, for many of today's modern families, Sunday has become a day to do many things, and in most of those families, God is not included on their itinerary. Sports, going to the beach, or going to special events is wonderful, but it is important to understand that when God becomes less important than our materialistic way of life, then the moral collapse of the family is predictable and unstoppable. In these worrisome times, the average secular family is not as 'tightly knit,' as it was in years ago. Parents who are diligent in overseeing their children's spiritual development, unfortunately, have become outdated.

If children are going to honor their parents, then there has got to be a family relationship, which begins with the recognition, the understanding, and the acceptance of the Laws of God. Otherwise, we, as a society will continue to see the morals and principles of youth continue to drop to an all time low. It is important for youths to be accepted by their peers, so parents, make sure that their peers have the same understanding and acceptance of God as you do. Be selective, for your children's sake.

It is common to hear people say, "Where did we go wrong"? "When did the world become so entrenched in a culture of violence, drug, and alcohol abuse, and an open rebellion of youth"? The answer is actually very simple. Although, some might say that it is too simplistic or not correct but I believe that it began when we "expelled" God from our daily life. The decay of moral values, in America began with the removal of prayer from school and the viewing of the Ten Commandments from public areas. The direct denial of the Ten Commandments, by our culture, has had a definite impact on the behavior and actions of the youth of America today. The Ten Commandments defines what is permissible and what is not permissible in our society today. The value of the Ten Commandments in our culture is priceless, because they build strong families and the family is the building block of our nation. We know that strong families will build a strong country, with strong leaders. However, we know the results when families are broken or flawed; we read about the tragic events in newspapers headlines every day.

Friends, life's journey passes through different stages. The way we honor our father and mother varies from stage to stage. It all seems to depend where the individual is on this journey called life. For example, you might be the child. You may be the parent. On the other hand, maybe you are in the middle, both the parent and the child. In any case, the way you honor your father and mother will vary from stage to stage. We need to be aware of where we are, on the path of life, so that we can best honor our parents, as they deserve. Whether we honor our parents by obeying them or by caring for them, they always deserve our dignity and respect. The example that we provide for our children as parents and ultimately as a society, will either enable honor and love from our children, or deter our children from honoring and caring for us as parents.

Words to Contemplate:

As a hospice chaplain for many years, I can truly tell you that death and separation always brings pain. Whether the death was expected, and everything was planned or not. I have noticed that people have two kinds of grief at the loss of a loved one. The first kind of grief is the pain of separation at death, with no regrets, except that which is caused by the separation. For example, the wife who lovingly took care of her husband during a long illness, or the adult child who always showed appreciation for his or her parents and never missed an opportunity to tell them of his or her love. Then there is a second kind of grief. The most painful and severe form of grief that I have seen people experience. These people mourn not only the loss of the one they loved, but also the pain of the broken relationship and lost time. This is the pain of the regret and the missed opportunities in a life, failure to repair their relationship, and failure to forgive. Sometimes the words "I love you" and "I'm sorry" only come when the casket is being closed. Do not let the breach of a relationship become too deep, that the pain later on becomes un-bearable.

I believe that the overpowering tears, which are shed over the graves of loved ones, are for words that were left unsaid and the deeds that were left undone.

Let us pray:

Holy and Almighty God, we are deeply grateful for Your great love for us. You have nurtured our souls with love, so in faith, we offer You all the hurtful experiences in our lives. Take them, and in turn, restore the harmony and peace in our hearts. Grant us the healing power of Your Son, Jesus Christ. May our hearts obey His calling, and may we follow Him. In Jesus Christ, we pray. Amen.

Parent's Prayer:

Heavenly Father, Make me a better parent. Teach me to understand my children. To listen patiently to what they have to say. And to answer all their questions kindly. Keep me from interrupting them or contradicting them, for I would not like it to be done to me. Forbid that I should ever laugh at their mistakes, or resort to shame or ridicule them if they displease me. Bless me, Father, with the bigness to grant them all their reasonable requests. And the courage to deny them privileges that I know will do them harm. Make me a fair and kind parent. I pray dear Lord that I will be worthy to be loved, respected, and imitated by my children in all that I say and do. Amen

Source Unknown.

6

Sixth Commandment of God

You shall not kill.
(**Exodus 20:13**).

Cain talked with Abel his brother, and it came to pass, when they were in the field, that Cain rose up against Abel his brother and killed him. Then the Lord said to Cain, "Where is Abel your brother"? He said, "I do not know. Am I my brother's keeper"? And He said, "What have you done? The voice of your brother's blood cries out to Me from the ground. So now you are cursed from the earth, which has opened its mouth to receive your brother's blood from your hand"

(**Genesis 4 8-11**).

The Sixth Commandment, "You Shall Not Kill," is recorded in Exodus 20:13. The Hebrew word for "Kill" is ratsach, but "murder" would be a more accurate translation. The term applies to the deliberate and willful act of terminating the life of another. This commandment is probably the most universally recognized law of God among religions around the world. This commandment outlines a basic principle that no one has the right to decide who should live and who should die. However, in our world today that is not the case. Unfortunately, we are living in a time when there is little or no regards for the sanctity of human life. God makes it extremely clear, that He wants us to respect our life and the life of other people as the greatest and most marvelous gifts of God. Therefore, in the light of this commandment, it should be obvious that committing suicide is also a grave transgression of the laws of God. Suicide is one form of murder. Included in suicide, is the sin of lack of faith, lack of trust, sin of despair, and rebellion against God's providence. Suicide is a very dangerous sin for the soul. Think about it, by terminating your own life, you are going to forfeit the very possibility of repentance of this sin, since after death; God does not accept repentance.

You see, humanity has been made in the complete image of God and has been given a mind so that he can glorify God, and be included in His eternal family. Although this world can bring us much suffering and despair, it is important to remember that suffering and despair, no matter how great, are only temporary, and if asked, God gives us the strength to bear even the most terrible situations during one's lifetime. Ultimately, God uses those situations to make us better and stronger believers in Him. Friends, remember that the path to heaven is a narrow and thorny one. The parable of the rich man and Lazarus clearly describes the meaning of earthly sufferings. Think about the rich man tormented in hell, and Abraham says to him, "Son remember that in your lifetime you received many good things, and likewise Lazarus evil things, but now he is comforted and you are tormented"(Luke 16:19-31).

While we endure suffering on this earth, know that God is extremely merciful, for those that trust and believe in Him, God will strengthen and console, and will not give more than what the soul can bear.

In the Sermon on the Mount, our Lord, Jesus Christ explains very clearly the ultimate cause of all violent actions against others. "You have heard that it was said to those of old, you shall not murder, and whoever murders will be in danger of judgment. But I say to you that whoever is angry with his brother is in danger of the judgment...You have heard that it was said, "An eye for an eye and a tooth for a tooth. But I tell you not to resist an evil person. But whoever slaps you on your right cheek, turn the other to him also. If anyone wants to sue you and take away your tunic, let him have your cloak also.....You have heard that it was said, "You shall love your neighbor and hate your enemy. But I say to you, love your enemies, bless those who curse you, do good to those who hate you, and pray for those who spitefully use you and persecute you, that you may be sons of your Father in heaven"(Mathew 5:21-40).

In the above passage reading note that three times Jesus Christ said, You have heard", followed by, "But I say." What Jesus was doing was actually making the Law more binding. Therefore, for those who call themselves Christians, followers of Christ, then the truth in these three verses will not be able to be explained away on judgment day.

It is clear to see that the greatest form of evil that can be done to one's neighbor is to take his or her life. However, it is just as serious to take one's own life. God created us and therefore, no man possesses such power that he is free, to bypass God, kill another, or put him to death. The Lord taught us that "the wages of sin is death" and so no murderer will have eternal life, with blood "still" on their hands. In other words, death without or before repentance of murder, will not provide one with eternal life.

Some believe that although this commandment forbids one to kill another, it might be lawful to kill oneself, under special circumstances, or that of an unborn child, still in its mother's womb. You see, man, under the direction of Satan, has devised clever ways to justify whatever they do, regardless of what God thinks of it.

Negotiations broke down in the attempt to pass the health care reform bill when Nancy Pelosi (D.CA), allowed Rep. Bart Stupack (D.MI) to introduce an amendment that would place additional restrictions on abortion funding legislation. Rep. Stupak wanted to secure that the language on the health care reform bill would strip abortion funding nationally. Under HR 3962, which is the current health care bill, abortions, are funded in two ways. First, through the public option and second, through the affordability credits given to consumers to purchase health care. Rep. Stupak said, "We're asking members to maintain current law and oppose federal funding on abortion."

Congressman Chris Smith, a New Jersey Republican who leads the pro-life caucus in the House, stated, "Abortion not only kills children, it harms women physically and psychologically and risks significant subsequent harm to future children. If we truly want to see fewer abortions and want to reduce them, then don't fund them."

Currently, pro-abortion lobbying groups are enjoying funding and support like never before in history. President Barak Obama along with his anti-life majority in Congress, organizations like Planned Parenthood are looking forwards to greater funding opportunities for the coming years. The abortion on demand agenda in America and overseas is massively expanding with our taxpayer's money. Citizens need to stand firm and oppose the murder of innocent unborn children. How do we do this you might ask? Know the facts. Know that there has been an increase in federal funding ($300 million last year) for Planned Parenthood, which is the organization that performs the most abortions in America. In addition, make sure that the Hyde Amendment remains as law. You see the Hyde Amendment is not a permanent law; instead, it is a "rider" that has been attached to annual appropriations bills since 1976.

As the abortion issue becomes the 'Achilles' heel of the Democratic Party, Democrats also have to defend and uphold the Constitution of the United States, which makes no reference to the right to have abortions subsidized by a federally funded program. Currently, the majority of the American people oppose establishing a federal program that will fund abortions on demand. Therefore, I believe, that since we live in a nation which is run "by the people and for the people", that the Democrats should listen to the American people, and do what is right according to God's law and to the law of men.

There are many methods of killing today, think about the never-ending stream of terrorist acts around the world from terrorist attacks to suicide bombings, and almost all of them in the name of "God" or "Allah." Think about the outright aggression due to religious differences, and the confiscating of the property of others fueling wars between nations. Think about the large-scale conflict, which brings, destruction of land to hunger, and from disease to death, even to genocide. Unfortunately, it becomes a never-ending retaliation of revenge and then, more war, more conflict, and more death. How do you think God feels about all these deaths, the deaths of innocent man, women, and children?

Nowadays the dilemma in the killing arena is, "is it going to be in the form of "weapons of mass destruction," or is it going to be nuclear, chemical or biological"? Are we going to destroy one part of the world, or most of it? In addition, can it be justified by world leaders or politicians in order to gain or keep their power or control? Regardless of their rationalization, God clearly says, "You shall not kill."

In America, however, the murders and killings are more subtle, and as stated before most murders are committed in the form of abortions. I was recently reading that each year about half of all the pregnancies among American women are unintended or unplanned, and out of those, about 1.3 million each year end in abortion. Yet with over 2 million families in America are wanting to adopt a child, there is no such thing as an unwanted child.

On the website of the late term abortionist, Dr. George Tiller, he claimed that he aborted roughly 2,009 post 15 weeks' fetuses. He claimed that late term abortions were in the best interest of the children that were aborted. He continued by saying that some of these babies had abnormalities such as Down's syndrome and cystic fibrosis reducing the level of their quality of life. However, the disposal of viable unborn babies, due to parental "inconvenience" or because it is not a "perfect" child does not permit murder to be committed. The argument often heard by the abortion industry is that such children, if they are allowed to live will pose a threat to the psychological well being of the mothers who will have to raise them and care for them. However, the real motivation behind any abortion, late term or not, is the destruction of an un-wanted fetus. Doctors that participate in such destruction of life will need to answer to God on judgment day. They have violated God's Sixth Commandment; **you shall not kill.**

It is interesting that many couples who cannot have babies

are going as far as China and Russia to adopt a newborn child, and yet here in the states, many of the same age babies are being dismembered, decapitated, and ultimately trashed at many local Planned Parenthood Clinics. What does this say about how we view the sacredness of a human life? How would the God of the Bible view such an action?

According to the 2009 pamphlet of Prolife America, a baby's heart begins to beat at 18 days. At 43 days, the brain coordinates movements and by 8 weeks, all organs are functioning. At 9 weeks, the baby has fingerprints. The sense of comfort and pain is obtained at 10 weeks, and the baby can smile, suck his/her thumb and make a fist by 12 weeks of life. It is clear that life begins at conception. Nobody has the right to terminate a life that God has created. The only exception to this would be if the life of the mother is at stake. Such incidents are quite rare with today's modern medicine.

As our government becomes more liberal and more politically correct, we notice that the President of the United States is making decisions, which go directly against the will of God, the laws of God, and the teachings of God.

Probably one of the worst decisions that President Obama has made to date, in regards to abortion, is voting against the "Born Alive Infants Protection Plan" (BAIPA). This Illinois bill would have protected infants who survived an abortion. You see, the induced labor abortion procedure, many times results in babies being born alive. Such babies are then left to die. Jill Stanek, a nurse, who supported BAIPA, discovered that infants, who survived abortions, were left to die in soiled utility rooms. Barack Obama stated that his opposition to this bill derived from a concern that this bill would be used to undermine the Roe vs. Wade decision and the Illinois state law concerning abortions. President Obama stated that he also opposed the bill because he believed that requiring a second doctor to assess and care for a baby that survived a botched abortion would be too distressing for the abortionist and upsetting for the woman who had the abortion. President Barack Obama voted against this bill twice in committee and once on the Senate floor. The bill was meant to provide protection for the babies who survived abortions, equal to the protection that a premature baby would receive.

Barak Obama not only opposed the bill all three times, but he was the only state senator to speak against the bill in 2002. The bill finally passed in 2005, after Barak Obama left the legislature.

Last year, there was an astonishing admission by the U.S. Supreme Court Justice Ruth Bader Ginsburg that was noted on the World Net Daily News. She says she was under the impression that legalizing abortion with the 1973 Roe vs. Wade case would eliminate the undesirable members of our society, or as she put it "populations that we don't want to have too many of". (World Net Daily, July 9, 2009). It looks like many in the leadership of our country, are "expelling" God and His laws, even at a federal level. Be assured that there will be a Final Judgment where God will separate the sheep from the goats forever.

The value that God places on an unborn child are described a couple of times in the Old Testament. In Exodus 21:22-23, it says, "If men who are fighting hit a pregnant woman and she gives birth prematurely but there is no serious injury, the offender must be fined whatever the woman's husband demands and the court allows. But if there is serious injury, you are to take a life for life." Here God is plainly saying that if you cause the death of an unborn child, then it should be treated the same as murder. In addition, in the Psalms we read of the high value that God places on the unborn child: "For you created my inmost being, you knit me together in my mother's womb. I praise you because I am fearfully and wonderfully made, your works are wonderful, I know that well. My frame was not hidden from you when I was made in the secret place. When I was woven together in the depths of the earth, your eyes saw my unformed body. All the days ordained for me were written in your book before one of them came to be" (Psalm 139: 13-16).

The majority of America does not support public funding for the legalized murder of the unborn child. Yet, our current administration was trying to include abortion in the health care bill. Let us face the facts, it is one thing to take a pro-choice position on the abortion issue, however, it is quite another to support an activity that one opposes in conscience. The Obama administration plans to fund the abortion industry with 1 billion dollars in taxpayer funds at the Federal and state level. If a person chooses to have an abortion, although it is murder, and against God's laws, it should be paid by the person who wants to have the abortion, not by everyone else. Especially those of us who oppose the practice in conscience.

Unfortunately, right to life advocates have lost their first battle in congress. The Health Care Reform Bill that passed on March 21, 2010, specified that individuals and families who receive federal subsidies to buy their main policies also could separately purchase insurance that will cover abortion if they use their own money to do so. I believe that this amounts to public financing of abortion because the subsidies will facilitate the purchase of the separate policy. The Congress of the United States essentially passed a bill that will advance the pro-abortion agenda in our country. Believe me, more abortions will be performed, the sanctity of life challenged, and once again our nation has forsaken its God and His commandment, "Thou shall not kill."

Now let us talk about another form of murder. We see an example of this in second Samuel.1. Here a man reports that when Saul was mortally wounded and dying, he killed him. King David, recognizing this as equal to murder, sentenced the man to death. When the jailer in Philipi was in despair and about to kill himself, Paul called out words, which apply to us also, "Don't harm yourself"(Acts 16:28).

Jack Kevorkian was born on May 26, 1928. By the age of seventeen, he had graduated from his high school with honors. Kevorkian continued with his education and graduated from Michigan Medical School in 1952 with a medical degree. Jack Kevorkian became a pathologist. However, that is not all of his accomplishments; Kevorkian is also an oil painter, jazz musician and composer, and flute and organ instrumentalist. This highly talented individual is, best known for his right to die agenda, via physician-assisted suicide. He claims that to date he must have assisted over one hundred and thirty patients commit suicide. Jack Kevorkian does not believe that there is a God or a Creator of the universe. So many talents to be thankful to God for, and yet, Kevorkian continues to deeply betray and slander God with his support of assisted suicide.

Kevorkian was tried many times for assisting people commit suicide, and ultimately he served an eight years prison term of his ten to twenty five year prison sentence for second-degree murder. His medical license was terminated for life. Kevorkian is currently on parole, and has become an advocate for assisted suicides. In fact, on September 2, 2009, he appeared on the Fox News Network, discussing health care reform and euthanasia. I am sure that Kevorkian is unaware, or maybe does not care, that in this commandment, God finds guilty of murder anyone that "promotes" the murder or allows someone else to do it. Personally, I consider euthanasia completely immoral in nature. For, as long as evil abides in people, as a society, we can expect escalating crimes in all areas of life. The only true solution to this problem of sin is the reformation of the human heart back to God. Unfortunately, I do not think our society, as a whole, is there yet.

Now, I would like to introduce you to what I consider another dangerous man, to world-civilized societies, a follower of Kevorkian, Philip Nitschke.

Dr. Philip Nitschke was born in 1947 in rural Australia. Nitschke obtained a PhD in Physics in 1972 and then graduated from Sydney University Medical School in 1988. Nitschke is highly known around the world. He is the founder of the pro-euthanasia group called Exit International. Just like Kevorkian, Nitschke provides advice and assistance to those who want to end their lives. One of Nitschke's cases that are more famous was that of Nancy Crick, only 69 years old when he assisted her in taking her life. With relatives and friends present, Ms. Crick took a lethal dose of barbiturates as instructed by Dr. Nitschke, who was not present at the time.

Nitschke is also well known for presenting a plan to launch a "death ship" which would euthanize people from around the world in international waters where he could by-pass restricted national laws.

In a 13 hour, paid television program, which promoted doctor assisted suicide, Nitschke lectured on end of life choices and voluntary euthanasia. This program was aired in Hong Kong and China on October 2009, called, "Dignified Departure." Here Nitschke stated that he believed that voluntary euthanasia should not only be available to the terminally ill, but basically to any elderly person who is afraid of getting old and being incapacitated. He spoke about the "peaceful pill" (Nembutal) which is revolutionizing the field of euthanasia in the same way that the contraceptive pill transformed birth control. During this program, Dr. Nitschke also explained and advocated to the public his reasoning for, what I call, direct and intentional killing of the depressed, handicapped, sick, elderly, and dying.

By condoning euthanasia or assisted suicide, our society will no longer find it to be their common duty, to protect the lives of the weakest in our society. Ultimately, the fear will be that euthanasia or assisted suicide will be imposed on individuals as a way to eliminate expensive treatments, and even to diminish the demands on the caregivers. This of course, would erode the trust that patients have on their family and caregivers, to say the least, and it would eventually cause isolation and fear in many members of our society. How many cases will we see of close family friends or relatives who might want to expedite the dying process due to personal gain from the death of the deceased? Unfortunately, this is a reality throughout the Netherlands, where euthanasia is legal, and thousands of patients are killed every year, sadly these mercy killings do not come from the patients themselves but from their families who, frankly, in many cases are trying to get rid of them.

Obama's health care reform bill, also known as "America's Affordable Health Choices Act of 2009" seniors are being told that the government will help them plan on how they want to die. On Section 1233, Page 424, the doctor would be paid for having a consultation with the patient on "advance care planning". However, patients do not have to be ill; instead, they just have to be over a certain age, which will suggest to the doctors that it is time to talk about death.

Our laws against assisted suicide are to protect the moral insight about the value of every human life. Such laws exist to protect the vulnerable and weak of our society and any erosion of such laws would carry with it great dangers. When a person is ill or disabled, are they any less deserving of the protection of our laws than anyone else?

Unfortunately, as our economy weakens, seniors may have to live on much meager funds in the future. Common problems associated with old age, like maybe getting hip replacement surgery, will cause one to consider end of life options, especially if the health care plan will not pay for the surgery, and one does not want to be a burden to their family.

It was almost one year ago, last November, that Washingtonians went to the polls and approved the "Initiative 1000" which is the Washington "Death with Dignity Act". It is interesting to note that this law is almost identical to the Oregon's assisted suicide law. Patients with a terminal illness are given a brochure by the "Compassion and Choices" or (C&C) which is the assisted suicide advocacy group, formerly called the Hemlock Society. This brochure then provides all the alternatives available to cancer patients and other patients with terminal diseases. From hospice care to assisted suicide, it is all there. The brochure goes on to explain how a volunteer from the C&C Society can assist in finding a doctor which will, "locate physicians who support a patient's choice to use the law", basically it really means finding a doctor who is willing to prescribe a deadly overdose of drugs.

The real issue is simply, "Who possesses the authority to take a human life"? That judgment is reserved for God, and God alone. The Sixth Commandment is very clear in reminding us that God is the giver of life, and that He alone has the authority to take it. Many times in the Bible, God has revealed His deep concern about the sanctity of the life He created. God sees the taking of a human life as an attack upon those who are made of "His Image" therefore; it becomes an indirect attack on God Himself.

Indeed our world has become more violent. On an international level, we are dealing with the present threats of nuclear, chemical, and biological warfare. On a national level, the rates of homicides and suicides have been steadily increasing at an alarming rate. Now we also have the "back-door" legalization of assisted suicide and euthanasia, a "death with dignity" campaign in many parts of the world, including our own United States.

We are presently living in a culture of death, something never experienced before in America. I know that seems hard to believe, but look around you. Read some of the new laws and directives, such as Washington's C & C brochure. At the same time that God is forbidding us to take life unjustly, God is also commanding us to protect it at all cost. It is time that collectively, as Americans, we support God and the sanctity for life.

If you are the kind of person that has broken the sixth commandment of God, there is hope for you. Repent and ask the Lord for forgiveness. Trust in the God of Creation, the soul you save might be your own.

Words to Contemplate:

Father, help us conquer the menace of evil which so easily takes root in the hearts of people today. And whose immeasurable effects is destroying our modern world.

From sins against human life from its very beginning, God, deliver us.

From demeaning of the dignity of all that are sick and elderly, God, deliver us.

From secular oppression against the Gospel of Jesus Christ, God deliver us.

From loss of awareness of good and evil, God deliver us.

From the readiness of secularism to trample on the Ten Commandments, God deliver us.

From the attempts to stifle in human hearts the truth of God, deliver us.

Father, may You stop evil, transform consciences, and reveal the power of the Holy Spirit to conquer all the "sins of the world." Amen.

Let us pray:

Almighty God, pour Your grace into our hearts. Oh Lord, we have sinned against You. Please, forgive us and give us the courage and strength to always bear witness to Your word. Heavenly Father, You are the God in whose Name the founders of this great country won liberty and freedom for. May we remain firmly grounded as a nation in truth, and grant that Your Ten Commandments be always honored by our nation's leaders. In Jesus Christ, we pray. Amen.

7

SEVENTH COMMANDMENT OF GOD

You Shall Not Commit Adultery.

"Marriage should be honored by all, and the marriage bed should be kept pure, for God will judge the adulterer and all the sexually immoral"
(Heb. 13:4).

"You have heard that it was said to those of old, "You shall not commit adultery. But I say to you that whoever looks at a woman to lust for her has already committed adultery with her in his heart"
(Mathew 5:27-28).

In an era were divorce is common, and sex seems to have no boundaries, the Seventh Commandment of God essentially focuses on infidelity, which, unfortunately, is now at epidemic proportions. In fact, infidelity studies confirm that most people will cheat on their marriage partner during their marriage. It seems to be that those who respect their marriage vows are the exception rather than the rule. With this commandment, God is joining the husband and the wife to preserve mutual fidelity. God is asking that our thoughts, feelings, and actions be pure in nature.

The Seventh Commandment, "You shall not commit adultery,"

is designed by God to guard the sanctity of the home. The sanctity of the family, you see, God gave us this commandment to direct the marriage couple into a loving, trusting, natural relationship that is meant to bring tremendous blessings to the family unit and to the community at large. Jesus makes it quite clear that God, intended marriage to be a monogamous and permanent relationship, divinely ordained and the root of generations to come (Matthew 19:3-6).

Today's world is saturated in an overflow of sexual pleasure, pursuit, and perversions. Whether it is in or out of marriage, many in our society are having a difficult time making a distinction between the true meaning of sex and marriage and all other forms of currently available sex-related activities. We are currently living in a time where there is essentially no limits on internet sites, cable television, movies, books, magazines, photographs, songs, and even advertisements that utilize pornography or sex related activities to promote their product. "Sex Sells," as one movie promoter puts it. In addition, sex without boundaries has become the mindset, which emphasizes that all sex is good, whether it is in or out of marriage. As moral barriers drop, there is no guilt, and anything goes. Have you seen the website for those who would like to have extra-marital sex without strings attached? The website will find someone close to where you live and both parties then arrange the sexual encounter. The only fee involved is to the website provider to join the group. Today it is common for the average person to go to a pornography website, in which with ease and privacy of their own home, they can purchase adult videos and toys of every kind. Experimentation and indulgences of every conceivable sexual act, has become the norm for many households. Even bestiality, which was witnessed in ancient times, is now reappearing in many cultures. The social and personal harm that this "revolution of sexual immorality" is causing is so invasive that it defies society's ability to quantify its toll on human suffering. However, most people refuse to acknowledge its staggering consequences.

Our current contemporary laws make it very easy to divorce your spouse and remarry another. Conversely, Christian spouses should always submit themselves to God, who instituted the bond of marriage and said, "What God has joined together, let no man separate" (Mathew 19:6). So, in light of God's commandment against adultery, how are people responding to it in today's society? During this past year, there were unbelievable amounts of infidelity stories in the news. It seems that Americans of all lifestyles were included on the "top ten" of the infidelity stories of the year. Yes, everybody was getting on the infidelity track. Politicians, sport figures, celebrities, and the rich and famous were cheating on their mates, setting an example for the rest of the nation. Probably the top infidelity news story of 2009 was the Tiger Woods infidelity scandal that began on a one-car accident on Thanksgiving Day, and it led to a revelation of the golfer's secret love life with as many as 18 alleged mistresses. Since the news of the scandal surfaced, there have been reports of million-dollar hush money payoff, possible divorce from his wife, Elin Nordegren, and entrance into a "sex addiction" clinic by Tiger Woods to get help for his addiction and to try to save his marriage. Tiger Woods told the media that there was a sense of "entitlement" that surrounded his reasoning for his affairs.

In the entertainment industry, we have people like David Letterman who was forced to confess to having sex with many female staff workers, especially his long sexual liaison with staffer Stephanie Birkitt. This dirty laundry was revealed when Birkitt's ex-boyfriend tried to use information found in Birkitt's diary to allegedly exhort money from David Letterman. Yes, Mr. Letterman, following the seventh commandment would have saved you a lot of trials and troubles.

The seventh commandment is every bit as relevant in modern America today as it was 3500 years ago at Mr. Sinai. This commandment prohibits sexual immorality of every kind and it teaches us to honor and follow God's plan for sexual fulfillment in marriage. That plan is very simple: It is one man and one woman married for life (Genesis 2:18-24).

Friends, here is the fundamental reality: Since the internet provides anonymity, accessibility, and affordability of sexual resources, the computer can accelerate the transition from "at risk" to "addicted" as well as to the progression of sex addiction in those with a history of prior sexual compulsivity. Dr. Bob Lanier at askbob. com says that 8-10 percent of internet users will become hooked on cybersex. Evidently, there seems to be a form of hypersexual online behavior that will definitely lead to real time infidelity. According to the Academy of Matrimonial Lawyers, spouses who are hooked on internet porn are a growing complaint among spouses filing for divorce, according to a survey of 350 divorce attorneys. This is just the tip of the iceberg; there is a lot more statistical data on the effects of infidelity. All you have to do in go online to see the immensity of the problem. It is a fact that the current percentage of the population who has had affairs today is quite high because infidelity and divorce are treated casually in our culture these days. Yet, God's view of divorce is far from casual. The world's expectation of marriage has become that of a "needless burden" however, that is not the way that Jesus addressed the topic of marriage and divorce in the Gospel. If you read Mathew 5:32, and 19:9, Mark 10:11-12, and Luke 16:18 you are going to get one single consensus: Basically, if a husband and wife divorce and either one remarries, that person is committing adultery against his or her spouse. The only exception that Jesus mentioned was sexual immorality, in which case he or she is free to remarry without the fear of breaking God's law.

One of the most emotional and public collapse of a marriage was that of John Edwards who cheated on his terminally ill, cancer stricken wife. In an ABC News "Nightline" interview, the former presidential candidate admitted lying about his extra marital affair with his videographer, Rielle Hunter, during his campaign for the presidency. Later on, it was released to the public that he was the father of her newborn baby.

Then there is former President Clinton and Monica Lewinsky. As I mentioned before, President Clinton lied under oath, swearing that he did not have a sexual affair with Ms. Lewinsky. It was revealed later that they did have an adulterous affair, especially when Ms. Lewinsky produced an item of clothing as evidence, which had a stain made by the President's semen.

The highly publicized divorce trial of supermodel Christie Brinkley and Peter Cook uncovered details about Peter Cook's affair with his teenage mistress and the exposure of his internet porn habit of $3000 a month. Mr. Cook ultimately revealed that his infidelity was a result of his sexual addiction that he has had for years.

Cybersex is really such an easy temptation, that Satan himself must have designed it. The internet offers a relative degree of anonymity and people can ease their way into affairs, starting out in chat rooms, deceiving themselves into thinking that they are in control, yet leading them down the path of temptation to infidelity. To grasp the scope of this problem, just take a look at the electronic surveillance software available, now being sold to monitor e-mails and daily internet activity. Attorneys recommend the use of electronic internet surveillance software to spy on your spouse or lover internet use. This information could someday be used in a divorce court.

God, of course, would want forgiveness and reconciliation in the marriage. However, repetitious infidelity may be the result of deviant character development, in which some people actually derive a perverted satisfaction from having many sexual conquests and deceiving their spouse. In this case, it might be advisable, that the individual be diagnosed and treated by a mental health professional. Much counseling needs to take place before any spiritual work can be effective in the marriage. Ultimately, forgiveness, through the grace of God, is the only way that one can find redemption after such intimate betrayal.

It almost seems as if the business of "lust" has replaced baseball or football as our nation's pastime. America seems to be obsessed by lust. I was reading that our country is one of the world's leaders in the production of pornographic videos. Americans spend billions of dollars a year on pay-per-view porn that is piped into their hotel room or into their living room. Then there are the pornographic magazines, videos, and even advertisements that use sex to sell jeans to soft drinks. A more controversial commercial is the one that features a young man wearing only his white, underwear. Yes, in today's society, sex does sell. Furthermore, prime time television pushes the envelope when it comes to sexual content and nudity. This is so regardless of the time slot given to the sexually explicit commercial.

The primary problem is that people are severely wounded emotionally, families go through a form of disconnection, and ultimately dissolve. Infidelity, regardless of the source, is ultimately destructive. It will destroy the core of the soul. As the Proverb states, "whoever commits adultery with a woman lacks understanding, he who does so destroys his own soul" (Proverbs 6:32). Imagine the psychological damage that an affair or a divorce can cause to the mind of a young, naive child. Or a child caught in the crossfire without any real form of psychological protection or assistance.

Yes, Satan knew exactly what he was doing when he planted the seed of infidelity in the mind of man. Once the enemy convinced humanity that wrong was right and that right was wrong, the sexual revolution was on. As Satan continues with his lies, so does the moral degradation of this nation. The rationalization of having an affair has become the norm for many individuals worldwide. Think about it, how many times have you heard someone say they had an affair because the "passion" had left the marriage. They were no longer interested in their partner, and sexually, they wanted someone different to bring back the excitement. Therefore, they leave their spouse and their children, move into a small apartment, because they cannot afford to pay for two homes, especially after the child support and alimony payments. The children are then raised in an economically disadvantaged one-parent household, sometimes remaining dependent on the welfare system even after they become adults. Unfortunately, for many children in our country, the story goes this way too often. Furthermore, a high percentage of children without fathers or from broken homes can end up in inner city gangs, as they search for the family that they do not have at home. Sometimes the disastrous effects can be crime and drug abuse. Ultimately, we all pay. The whole society suffers and that is why divorce is a major player in America going godless.

Modern western society, and even other European societies around the world, offers its people a new concept of political correctness. This concept embraces the mindset that allows people, sometimes-complete families, to live in whatever lifestyle they choose, "as long as it doesn't hurt anyone else." This form of mentality has perpetuated this age of excessive tolerance in many areas of our society. All forms of sexual sins such as stated in the bible, can have grave lasting effects on the children of our modern world. McKenzie Phillips, daughter of John Phillips, of the Mammas and the Pappas, recently came out with her autobiography in which she explains how ultimately it became "normal" for her, to be her father's sexual partner. Pedophilia is apparently far more common than we would like to believe here in America.

God created the family unit as a way to train children to obey and honor their parents, so that they will honor and obey God. God has given us the characteristics to properly nurture and care for our children. We are to teach our children to be loyal and obedient to God's words as stated in the Holy Bible. In addition, we are to follow the Ten Commandments as a means to ingrain faithfulness to God. However, between the extra-marital affairs and the sexual deviancies, society is quickly losing sight of what families are all about.

Furthermore, think of the consequences of sexual sins physically and emotionally. Consider the explosion of sexually transmissible diseases also known as STD's, and consider all the lives that AIDS has claimed throughout the years. Think of all the suffering that this form of lifestyle has brought about; when intimate, personal relationships are desecrated by deceptive partners.

The penalty of sin is death. In Leviticus, 20:10 reads, "And the man that commits adultery with another man's wife, even he that commits adultery with his neighbor's wife, the adulterer and the adulteress shall surely be put to death." God promised swift and severe punishment for those who committed adultery. They became an example used to instill fear in others.

Besides death as explained above, sin also produces two deadly effects that manifest themselves slowly, and in time. The first is a damaged relationship with God. In Isaiah 59:1-2 it shows that sin creates a division between God and humanity since the breach of trust has been broken. The "covenant" with God has been fractured and the terms that were agreed upon, by both God and humanity had dissolved. Can God trust a society that commits adultery and infidelity? Only through repentance and God's merciful forgiveness and love can the covenant be healed. The second deadly effect is the evil that it produces in our lives and in the world. The act of infidelity, for example, indirectly, produces complete family devastation for years to come.

In the New Testament, Jesus Christ taught that marriage was sacred and binding. When the Pharisees asked Jesus about the bill of divorcement that Moses had allowed, Jesus replied, "Moses because of the hardness of your hearts suffered you to put away your wives, but from the beginning it was not so. And I say to you, whosoever shall put away his wife, except it be for fornication, and shall marry commits adultery: and who so marries her who is put away does commit adultery." I believe that the most powerful statement on adultery by Jesus Christ is found in Mathew 5:27-28: "You have heard that it was said by them of old time, you shall not commit adultery: But I say unto you, that whosoever looks on a woman to lust after her has committed adultery with her already in his heart." Jesus expanded and magnified the Law of God so that it would be more binding as one's own thoughts had to be controlled.

All right friends, we know the sins, the consequences of sexual transgressions, the social and personal harm brought about from such forms of immorality. So how do we avoid such sins in this modernized world? There are four rules to keep in mind. First, ask yourself, and do not rationalize "Would God be pleased with my actions"? Secondly, make a covenant with your eyes and ears. Do not pollute your senses with what you see or hear. Thirdly, be observant of your thoughts. Satan will use temptation to lure you into his trap. Fourthly, pray, pray, pray. Ask God to keep you pure of heart, for your sake and the sake of your family.

On March 21, 1991, Jesus stated these words to Nancy Fowler, regarding this commandment. "Keep your thoughts, words, deeds, pure. Keep your thoughts, words, deeds, on Me. I am Holy. Stay close to Me. Call to Me for help."

Then on March 22, 1991 Jesus said, "Many souls are freely choosing to live in darkness. They think their decision is just for a few years on earth, but it is for all eternity. Many souls are plunging into eternal fires and are damned for all times. Most are there because of sins of the flesh. Those who willfully choose to murder are there with them. Repeated willful and impure thoughts, words, and deeds are sending people to eternal fires of darkness. My children are making a conscious decision to break My commandment. They repeat this sin then rationalize it and, then no longer recognize it as sin. I will banish these souls from My sight. I am the God of mercy and love and a just judge. Violation of My commandments kills the life of the soul. Woe to this wicked, sinful, generation. How quick you are to cease your prayers of peace the moment you think your peace is achieved. The anger of God the Father is mounting. Woe be My people who march with murderers, the abortionists. Woe to My priests who engage in impure acts. You have seen enough. You have heard enough. I have spoken"(Conyers Our Loving Mother Official Website for Nancy Fowler).

Remember Jesus has set us free to enjoy a life of complete fullness and joy. You can put the past behind you and come to God in repentance. It does not even matter what sexual sin you may have committed. Remember what Jesus said to the prostitute, "Neither do I condemn you, go and sin no more." It is time to embrace God's truth and renounce Satan's lies.

Yes, infidelity is every married person's worst nightmare, since betrayal of such intimate love is painful and anger inducing at times. The psychological cost is high, as millions of people are submerged into depression, and bitterness leading to a lack of self worth, confidence, and hope. Which many times contribute to all sorts of tragedies including suicides? However, remember that Jesus Christ was betrayed Himself, and through His love, He made redemption available to us all. Stay close to God and allow Him to heal you. Then and only then can you look at helping to heal others.

If we say we have no sin, we deceive ourselves, and the truth is not in us, but if we confess our sins, God who is faithful and just, will forgive our sins and cleanse us from all unrighteousness (1 John 1:8).

Words to Contemplate: Psalm 23 Explained.

The Lord is my Shepherd. (That's a relationship)
I shall not want. (That's supply.)
He makes me lie down in green pastures. (That's rest.)
He leads me beside the still waters. (That's refreshment.)
He restores my soul. (That's healing.)
He leads me in the path of righteousness. (That's guidance.)
For His name sake. (That's purpose.)
Yes, though I walk through the valley of the shadow of death. (That's testing.)
I will fear no evil. (That's protection.)
For You are with me. (That's faithfulness.)
Your rod and Your staff comfort me. (That's discipline.)
You prepared a table before me in the presence of my enemies. (That's hope.)
You anointed my head with oil. (That's consecration.)
My cup runneth over. (That's abundance.)
Surely goodness and mercy shall follow me all the days of my life. (That's blessing.)
And I will dwell in the house of the Lord. (That's security.)
Forever. (That's Eternity.)

Let us pray:

Dear Merciful God, whose mercy is everlasting, hear the supplications of your people. We give You thanks for bestowing upon Your people the forgiveness of sins, and for having raised us all into a new life of grace. Through the gift of the Holy Spirit, sustain us and give us a discerning heart, so that with a deep spirit of love towards You, we may always walk in Your ways. In Christ we pray, Amen.

8

EIGHT COMMANDMENT OF GOD

You Shall Not Steal. (Exodus 20:15).

This commandment is a direct order from God to respect the property of others. Transgressions against this commandment include, but are not limited to robbery, theft, extortion, fraud, and sacrilege, which is to misuse the funds that belong to the church. In essence, the longing for possessions makes people greedy. Jesus tried to counter act this passion of men. He said: "Do not lay up for yourselves treasures on earth, where Moth and rust destroy and where thieves break in and steal. Instead, lay up for yourselves treasures in heaven, where neither moth nor rust destroys and where thieves do not break in and steal"
(Mathew 6:19-20).

Everyone knows that stealing is wrong. To steal means to take something that does not belong to you. Even people who do not read the Bible know the Eight Commandment of God, "it is wrong to steal." So on the surface this seems to be an easy commandment to obey, and one in which there is little disagreement on. Yet, the prohibition on stealing can be quite extensive. You see, there are many different types of stealing, and some stealing is even done by people who consider themselves "God fearing" people. Unfortunately, in today's modern society, stealing can take many forms and it is not always easy to identify.

When we think of stealing, most people will think of shoplifting, since it is probably one of the most common forms of stealing in modern time. According to the National Shoplifting Prevention Coalition and the National Learning and Resource Center, more than $13 billion dollars worth of goods are stolen from retailers every year. That is breaks down to more than $35 million dollars per day. Only 25% of the shoplifters are children, the rest are adults. This averages out to approximately 27 million shoplifters in our nation today or 1 in 11 people. As our economy continues to plunge, more people are unemployed and struggling to make ends meet. There is a greater degree of anxiety and depression in our society, which according to many professionals, is the root cause of this kind of crime.

Here are more facts: Shoplifters steal from all kinds of stores and there really is no specific profile of a typical shoplifter. Shoplifters say that they are caught only once in forty eight times, and only 3% of the shoplifters are what law enforcement call "professionals." The majority of the shoplifters are people who really do not steal out of financial need or even greed, but as a reaction to the social and personal pressures incapacitating them in their daily life.

However the famous and the rich, who seem to have it all together, also shoplift. Just ask around Hollywood. Celebrity or affluent shoplifting is many times due to having a sense of entitlement. Celebrities such as Winona Ryder who stole $4,760 dollars worth of clothing and hair accessories from a Saks of Fifth Avenue store, supermodel Elle who has admitted from stealing from stores such as Macy's and Bloomingdale, and tennis star Jennifer Capriati who spoke candidly about her 1993 shoplifting arrest, all express being anxious and depressed when they stole the merchandise. Some professional are now stating that it is the feelings of self-entitlement, and the heart pounding rush of greed and fear that keeps many people shoplifting until the police catches them. Others continue to shoplift because they say that it is the exhilaration of the act that keeps them shoplifting repeatedly. "It's a kind of a rush that's hard to reproduce in any other way," they say.

It is disheartening the amount of stealing that goes on in our society today. Wrongful taking of someone else's property is on the rise, especially in the workplace. Many employees will not think twice about stealing from their employers. Bringing home office supplies, using office equipment such as copier, computers, or making long distance telephone calls for personal use is common practice today for many. Did you know that on the average, employees are productive only six hours in an eight hour work day? Consider also those who fail to put in a full day's work by taking time to surf the Internet, talk in chat rooms, send e-mails to friends, or idling their time away by playing computer games on their work computer. What about coming to work late, leaving early, or taking extended lunches? How about the extra coffee breaks and all that time spent around the water cooler? Friends, when people do this, it is a transgression of this commandment. We are children of God, and we understand and recognize that there are many ways of stealing that are not necessarily illegal. "One who is slack in his work is brother to one who destroys"(Prov.18:9). Being lazy or careless at work is equal to stealing what we may have appeared to earn.

However, let me assure you that employers do get even. In fact, it is common for the employer to demand longer hours of work and to reorganize or cut back on their work force to improve their profits. All of it done at the expense of their overworked and overstressed workers.

Modern theft encompasses many different kinds of crimes against both person and property. When you consider larceny, which is the wrongful taking of personal property, it includes con games, frauds, price altering, and even inside trading.

The Bernie Madoff investment scandal is better known as the Ponzi scheme of the former NASDAQ chairperson. Charges included security fraud, investment fraud, mail fraud, wire fraud, money laundering, perjury, and even stealing from an employee benefit plan. His penalty, 150 years in prison and $170 billion dollars in restitution. In his court pleading, Madoff admitted to being guilty of all criminal acts against his clients. According to the New York Daily News, Madoff said on the day that he was sentenced, "I have left a legacy of shame, as some of my victims have pointed out, to my family and my grandchildren. This is something I will live with for the rest of my life. I'm sorry." Madoff was then taken to the Butner Federal Correctional Complex in North Carolina where he will spend the rest of his life. There, I am sure that Mr. Madoff will have plenty of time to contemplate on his actions and their consequences. Will he find God there?

I believe that society has forgotten what stealing really is. There are so many ways to steal and so many ways to rationalize such stealing that the behavior becomes non-recognizable for many. And yet, like the rest of God's Commandments, the Eighth Commandment has deep spiritual significance because when we take something that does not belong to us, by whatever means we do it, we "sin" against our God as well as our neighbor.

Stealing is a grave sin and it breaks the covenant with God in two very distinct ways. First, God wants us to have confidence and trust in Him. Stealing says to God that you have no confidence in Him, and that you do not trust in His provision. Secondly, every theft is a theft against God because God is the One who gave the provision to others. You see God wants us to have confidence in Him and in the future, that He will provide for us. The Word of God is full of promises concerning the Kingdom of Heaven and the life to come. If we truly believe this, then we should trust that He will provide. Furthermore, His Kingdom is not of this world, therefore, we should invest our time in acquiring the spiritual riches that are eternal, and no one can take those from you.

Not long ago I read a study conducted by the University of Colorado regarding what makes people happy. Interestingly but not surprising, it was noted that material purchases or goods did not make people happy, instead life experiences and relationships did. Joy is obtained from meaningful experiences because such experiences become part of one's identity. In other words, you will get more joy out of taking a trip with your spouse, than buying gold. Furthermore, you can share stories of your trip, possibly show a video of the trip and save it for future generations. However, what can you say about a gold coin, and what will it say about you after you are gone?

Friends, material wealth is not the gauge that is used to measure success in life. Some say that it is measured by the degree of personal and spiritual development and the impact that it has had on family, friends, and community. Certainly, all of the above are extremely important, but what really matters is that one acquires a strong faith in God and trust in His providence for us. You see, God does want us to have possessions, He is the One that gives them to us, and this commandment protects us against losing them.

Since material wealth or goods do not measure success, then why do so many people steal? The reason that stealing is such a big problem today, at all levels, is that more and more people do not know the God of the Bible. We live in a time in which we are bombarded with information about new and better things creating a "if I don't have it, I must need it society." Since America wants to be politically correct, very little is said publicly about the God's Eighth Commandment. Only the thought of imprisonment keep most people from stealing in America today, not a place called Hell.

Let me share the story of a well-known pastor in Florida, and his shameful downfall from fame. This pastor had a growing congregation, the respect of his flock, and many ministries doing the Lord's work in the community. With a large congregation came large amounts of money for the church, and a lot of it went into the pastor's private account. However, the pastor rationalized his deed by saying that he put in many extra hours at the church for many years. During one of the pastor's trips overseas, for ministry purposes, of course, the church administrators conducted an audit by a local CPA firm. The audit clearly proved that the pastor was taking church money. The church administrators decided to press charges and to terminate the pastor's employment. While overseas, the pastor became quite ill from food poisoning and had minor heart attack. During this event, the pastor had a near death experience. In his NDE, the pastor came face to face with Jesus, and Jesus showed him where he would be spending eternity if he did not confess and make retribution to the church. When the pastor returned to Florida, he faced a possible jail sentence and termination of his job. However, since he cooperated with the police and confessed to his wrong doings, his sentence was lowered to house arrest, he made retribution payments to the church, and offered community service in homeless shelters. Currently, this pastor is working with the homeless population in South Florida. Unfortunately, his marriage did not survive the stress of his sin, the marriage ended one year later. We cannot turn away from God's teaching and think that there will be no consequences for our actions.

As we shift away from the Judeo/Christian moral values, we are shifting away from the very foundation of Western civilization. If you do away with prayers in school and in the public arena, if you do away with the Ten Commandments, if you do away with the Bible, then the consequences are a corrupt and immoral society. With such a society comes outright stealing and all forms of injustice. It all becomes justified in the end. Remember, the wrong becomes the right, and soon, the right will become un-identifiable.

Christ taught us earthly wealth was not to be the focus of men; instead, He said to accumulate spiritual treasures, which will have lasting value beyond the limitations of space and time. You see, God will not force His ways or purpose on anyone. Since we have free will, it is up to us to choose God's way.

Today in our nation and nations around the world humanity is plagued with business practices that are the direct opposite of what this commandment teaches. If I were to write down all the ways that "stealing" is done today, there would not be enough room in this book for anything else. Nevertheless, to continue with the more prevalent ones, think about the manufactures that make false claims in order to trick buyers into unnecessary purchases. There has to be literally hundreds of info commercials, which promise consumers hair restoration, weight loss, exercise equipment, or a pill or vitamin that will increase sexual energy. Most of them deceive the consumer into purchases of products that do not do what they promise to do. These practices essentially rob the consumers of their hard-earned money. This is stealing in a large scale and it is carried on everyday around the globe. Unfortunately, those misleading ads tend to affect the weak; the needy; and elderly of our society the most.

Consider the packaging in your local grocery store. Greedy for profits, manufactures are giving you smaller quantities in smaller packages; and the consumer is being overcharged for the real value of the product or food item. I am sure you noticed how the ice cream containers are getting smaller, and yet you are paying the same or more at the checkout counter. Stealing from others is a sin, regardless of the conditions. Understand this; God hears the cries of the defrauded employees and consumers.

So here is the point, when you steal from another individual, you are stealing from God also. Since God is not real to many people in our society, such people fail to see Him as the actual and rightful owner of all. Friends, God owns the earth and the universe, and God placed all the elements and materials needed by men to produce wealth. If a man produces much wealth in his lifetime, then God would require him to learn to share his excess wealth by giving to others.

Make no mistake about it. "You shall not steal," are God's words not men. In the New Testament, Paul wrote, "He who has been stealing must steal no longer, but must work, doing something useful with his own hands, that he may have something to share with those in need" (Ephesians 4:28). So here we learn that God wants us to obtain what we need by earning it, and how God intends for our neighbor to have what they need, is by our sharing with them. God is saying that we should be honest, generous, and charitable.

In this chapter, I have tried to outline several ways in which man is currently breaking this commandment of God, "You shall not steal." You see, everything in the world belongs to God; we are simply his managers, using what He entrusts to us in the ways that He desires. This discussion of the eighth commandment is not complete until we address the ways that we are stealing from God.

So how do we steal from God today? Well, first of all, as a nation we do not acknowledge Him on the Sabbath. We do not spend time with Him, in prayer, contemplation, meditation, or in Scripture. Most people neglect to pray to God daily; only in times of trouble do they call upon Him. There are people who call themselves a Christian and fail to live up to what that name implies. Are you thirsting for worldly pleasures and material goods? Do you believe in the "prosperity gospel" as the pastor whose story I shared with you? Are you honest, unselfish, and merciful? Do you renounce personal possessions as one of your Christian virtues? Remember what Jesus said to the young man, "If you want to be perfect, go and sell what you have and give it to the poor and you will have treasures in heaven, and come and follow me"(Matthew 19:21). I understand that not everyone is seeking perfection, but it is important not to place too much value on the things of this world. I believe that the fulfillment of this commandment includes contentment with what God has chosen to give us, and a good manager of those things.

It is now the time in which this earth is growing critically worse with calamities, wars, violence, plagues, and natural disasters, so it is important to know the "truth." Whether it is popular in our society or not, the truth came be found in the Ten Commandments of God. As I have stated before, America was founded on religious principles and it was plain to see that the founding fathers did in fact mix religion and politics in order to keep America a moral and ethical nation under God. Currently, the outlawed postings of the Ten Commandments in public places is just one more example of the increasingly hostility towards the Judeo/Christian value system.

As secular society tries to misguide people by calling evil good and good evil, as stated in Isaiah 5:20, America will see a dramatic shift away from the morals and values that made this country great. Friends, many prophecies are coming alive today before our eyes. While many in secular society focus on the changing of America into a politically correct nation, they are blind to see were these changes will lead our nation. Remember, the Bible is clear on what lies ahead. The message here today is a wakeup call to men and women who love the Lord. Take a stand for God. Invest your time and energy in obtaining the spiritual treasures that will last eternally. They are treasures that no thief can steal.

The treasures of the mind and soul are certainly, what God wants us to concentrate our energies on. On April 12, 1991, Nancy Fowler prophesized regarding what Jesus had told her about the eighth commandment. He said, "My dearest daughter, I will teach you about stealing, begin to write. Anytime that you are dishonest you are stealing. Dishonesty hurts the soul, yourself, and others…" "No one robs another without robbing Me. You will stand accused before Me. Repent, repent, repent"… "I have no thieves in My Kingdom. My Kingdom is not of this world. Nancy, all My commandments are rules of love. Fail in love and you fail in My Kingdom" (Conyers Our Loving Mother-Messages-10 Commandments).

Our nation has received much grace from God, but now as a large segment of our American society describes them as "spiritual but not religious," we see that people are making a real attempt to distance themselves from anyone or anything that is considered "religious" in any way. This is especially true for the Ten Commandments of God. Many in the secular world find them to be dogmatic and a threat to their constitutional rights. So they are banished from courtrooms, schools, TV, and general public arenas. Why is God such a threat? Because people without God, find contentment in the lack of accountability for their transgressions against Him. God then becomes an "inconvenient truth." A reminder of what is morally right and acceptable by our society and by God.

When one loves God and wants to please Him, he will not steal. The desire to steal is defeated by the desire to do good for God. Nevertheless, the greatest comfort of all is when Jesus was dying on the cross and the thief said, "Jesus remember me when you come into your kingdom"(Luke 23:42). Jesus then filled with love and compassion gave the thief the answer that He gives everyone who has broken the Law of God and turns to Him in repentance and faith: "You will be with me in paradise"(Luke 23:43).

Words to Contemplate:

I had a dream that I had an interview with God. "Come in," God said. "So you would like to interview Me?"

"If You have time," I said.

God smiled and said, "My time is eternity and it is enough to do it all.

"*Ok*" *I said. First question, "what surprises you most about humanity?"*

God answered:

That they get bored of being children, are in a rush to grow up, and then long to be children again.

That they lose their health to make money and then lose their money to restore their health.

That by being anxious about the future, they forget the present, such that they live neither for the present nor the future.

That they live as if they will never die, and they die as if they had never lived."

Then God took my hands and we were silent for a while, enjoying this special moment. I thanked Him for His time and I praised Him for His creation. And with a twinkle in His eyes and a smile on His face He asked me, "By the way, have you read my number one best seller?" "I've gotten some pretty good reviews. I hope everyone knows that there will be a test." God

Let us pray:

Oh Lord, we are deeply sorry that we have offended You. Whether in thought, word, or deed, we have not loved You with our whole heart. We are truly sorry and we humbly repent. Dear Lord, our faith teaches us that Your blood will cleanse our soul and we will become a new creation. Jesus, Son of God, we place our confidence in You. Bring us to the throne of grace that we may stand flawless before Your presence, and receive the "free gift" of eternal life. So that we may worship You now and forever. Amen.

Let's Remember Jesus as we recite the Anima Christi:

Soul of Christ, sanctify me. Body of Christ, heal me. Blood of Christ, drench me. Water from the side of Christ, wash me. Passion of Christ, strengthen me. Good Jesus, hear me. In your wounds, shelter me. From turning away, keep me. From the evil one, protect me. At the hour of my death, call me. Into your presence lead me. To praise you with all the saints, forever and ever. Amen. (Anima Christi).

9

Ninth Commandment of God

You shall not bear false witness.
(Exodus 20:16).

"His truth endures to all generations"
(Psalm 100:5).

"You say rightly that I am King. For this cause I was born, and for this cause I have come into the world, that I should bear witness to the truth. Everyone who is of the truth hears my voice"

(John 18:37).

"When we put bits into the mouths of horses to make them obey us, we can turn the whole animal...likewise the tongue is a small part of the body, but it makes great boasts. Consider what a great forest is set on fire by a small spark......all kinds of animals, birds, reptiles, and creatures of the sea are being tamed and have been tamed by man, but no man can tame the tongue"

(James 3:3,5,7-8).

It was with incredible power that God spoke from Mount Sinai, "You shall not bear false witness against your neighbor." (Exodus 20:16) This is the fifth of the commandments related to preserving loving relationships among humanity. Remember, as I said earlier, the first four commandments show us how to love God, while the last six explain how to love other human beings. With this commandment, God also teaches man how to protect his most important quality, his reputation. This commandment forbids all forms of lying, which can cause great harm to all involved. This would include slander, gossip, half-truths, deceptions, distortions, and perjury in court, false complaints, gossip, or any other statement that is said with the intention of lying. Respect for the reputation and honor of an individual is of upmost importance. Therefore, we should not judge others, always try to remember that we each have our own weaknesses, and we certainly do not want to be judged.

Truth or truthfulness is one of the virtues of God that consists of showing oneself true in deeds and in words without any hypocrisy. "If a man vow a vow unto God, or swear an oath to bind his soul with a bond, he shall not break his word, he shall do according to all that proceeded out of his mouth." (Numbers 30:2) There is a great gravity in an oath made in the name of God. Since truthfulness is a problem in our society, courtrooms across the nation will request that you place your hand on the Bible and swear in the name of God that your testimony will be truthful. This commandment is especially relevant for our system of justice for the Bible warns man several times that it is better not to vow than to vow and break your word. Although this commandment is mandatory in the legal arena, it is also necessary for daily life.

This commandment, like many of the others, needs to be kept not only with our words but also with our thoughts and actions. For example, prejudice, discrimination, injustice, intolerance, and bigotry are just some of the words that describe the action of "making assumptions about people based on outward appearances." In John 7:24 we read, "Stop judging by mere appearances, and make a right judgment."

In today's society, the temptation to lie never seems to cease.

Lying has become categorized and a way of life for many. Consider the little white lie, the stretching of the truth, the distortion of facts, and the exclusion of facts or information. For example, most people say that it is ok to lie on job applications, or to your boss, or to your spouse, or even to your friends. However, it is not ok to lie under oath, in a court of law. You see, lying has become a quick and effortless way to escape guilt, fear, or embarrassment. Lying is also a good way to get out of trouble" was the number one statement made, not by adolescents, but by adults in reference to their jobs.

In the New Testament, Jesus makes several statements governing our use of words: "Again, you have heard that it was said to the people long ago, "Do not break your oath but keep the oath you have made to the Lord. But either I tell you, do not swear at all, by heaven, for it is God's throne, or by earth, for it is His footstool, or by Jerusalem, for it is the city of the Great King. Do not swear by your head, for you cannot make even one hair white or black. Simply let your "yes" be "yes" and your "no" be "no." Anything beyond this comes from the evil one" (Matt. 5:33-37).

Unfortunately, bearing false witness has become an international pass time with the help of the World Wide Web. It appears that it is no big deal to slander someone that you do not even know half way across the world, and completely ruin his or her reputation. It is quite a revelation to go into forums or blogs and read awful character "assassinations" on an unsuspecting target. This deceitful practice of slanderous gossip is not just for a select group." Anyone can be a victim and be under attack, all it takes is a person with hate in his heart for a malicious rumor to take a life of its own. Think of the recent cases of teenagers who have committed suicide due to malicious bullying and character assassinations online. In James 3:6 we read, "See how great a forest a little fire kindles!" "The tongue is a fire, a world of iniquity. The tongue is so set among our members that it defiles the whole body, and sets on fire the course of nature; and it is set on fire by hell."

President Barack Obama, recently participated on an online town hall meeting, organized by liberal religious activists, for an audience of religious voters. The focus was to dispel any misinformation regarding the new health care reform bill. At one point, the President accused opponents of the health care bill as "bearing false witness" against his plans. "I know there's been a lot of misinformation in this debate. There are some folks out there who are, frankly, bearing false witness." Obviously, the President knows the impact in quoting the Ninth Commandment to a church going audience will aid his cause. However, the President must have forgotten to speak on a commandment earlier on the list, "You shall not murder," this in relation to his pro-abortion stand. The President's statement was made in direct reference to the debate about government funding of abortion on the health care bill. Regrettably, the President misused this commandment, since his critics are not lying, but essentially disagreeing with his plan for national health care plan that federally funds abortion.

God is the source of truth, and therefore, He requires that His people always speak truthfully. It was under God's inspiration that King David wrote, "Lord, who may dwell in your sanctuary? Who may live on your holy hill? He whose walk is blameless and who does what is righteous, who speaks the truth from his heart and has no slander on his tongue, who does his neighbor no wrong and casts no slur on his fellow man...(and) who keeps his oath even when it hurts." (Psalm 15:1-3 NIV). God expects that truth will become a way of life for all.

It seems that lying has become an acceptable way of life these days for many people, even President's feel that it is ok to tell a lie. I remember seeing the serious face of the former President Clinton, staring right into the camera, and with a sincere look that denied charges that, he had been involved sexually with Monica Lewinsky. The more that he denied it, the more the truth began to surface. Finally when the lie was revealed, President Clinton brought shame and discredit upon himself, his family, and the office of the President of the United States. The Bible warns us: "Be sure your sin will find you out,"(Numbers 32:23).

Satan can also lie and use trickery to lure us to lie. In Genesis, we read that Eve told Satan firmly, "God has said, You shall not eat it, nor shall you touch it, lest you die."(Genesis 3:3) Eve understood what God had said, she knew the truth. Then Satan deceived her by telling her a lie that Eve choose to believe. He said, "You shall not surely die" (Genesis 3:4). You know the rest. That was the first human sin ever committed. It was a lie that continues to echo our sinfulness with humankind today. Yet, today, lying is not taken seriously. Actually, it is condoned in many circles and for many situations. However, be advised that God has given humankind fair warnings about where our lies will lead us. Aside from bringing chaos in the real world, it will also offend God and ultimately, your covenant with God will be ruined.

This Commandment, like the others, needs to be kept in our thoughts, not just in our words. For example, prejudice and discrimination begins as thought and become action, when wrong and sometimes-foolish assumptions are made about superficial differences in people. Jesus said that we are not to judge others. What Jesus meant here is that only God can look into a person's heart, we cannot, so we must not judge based on mere appearances. Ultimately, we are all children of God, unique and special in His creation.

In America today, whether it is in business, politics or religion, "truth" has been replaced with "politically correct" information. It is almost impossible to be certain today of who is telling the truth. It seems that in almost every facet of life, individuals, businesses, politicians, and other organizations have become amazingly creative when seeing how deceptive they can be. As lying becomes an accepted way of life, we can relate to Isaiah's description of ancient Israel in Isaiah 59:4 "No one calls for justice nor does any plead the truth. They trust in empty words and speak lies; they conceive evil and bring forth iniquity." God expects truth to permeate every facet of our lives and our society. How can we restore this way of life again here in America? It begins with every one of us insisting to accept, believe, and speak the truth. The "way of truth" in this society is not an easy one, since human nature is deceitful in itself, but it is the one taught and mandated by God. With courage, self-discipline, and God's grace, we can rise above the weaknesses of human nature and overcome deceit.

Remember even the "Beloved" disciple of Jesus Christ did not possess the character needed to perfectly follow the Ten Commandments. For he was self-assertive, ambitious for honor, argumentative and resentful at times. However, the thing is that when we come to Jesus in total trust and faith, willing to do what He commands, all of His holiness becomes available to meet our needs. Whatever those needs may possibly be. We are all sinners, and our need is infinite. However, so is the grace of our Lord, Jesus Christ. In Jesus, be assured, that all of God's requirements are met. Therefore, we can all be transformed and united with Him, the King of Heaven, for all eternity, if we follow His laws.

Words to Contemplate:

Even the poorest, most abandoned person can experience the transforming power of God's grace. This is the good news of the Gospel. Not just that we will be happy with God in the afterlife, but that we can be happy with God right now, however desperate our situation is. Christianity is not about rules and laws, guilt and fear of punishment, or extrinsic rewards. It is about grace. The experience of God's transforming love and power in our lives that elevates and perfects our natural abilities and allows us to do more than we thought possible. In this sense, the life of every fully converted Christian moves beyond naturalism. It is God's grace that makes the Christian practice of everyday life possible. And it is this same power of grace that one day will bring us to the resurrection, the ultimate transformation of nature, and eternal life with God. (T. Nichols, The Sacred Cosmos, 2003)

Let us pray:

Father of compassion and mercy, we ask forgiveness for our sins. Strengthen us in times of adversity, so that we may walk in righteousness. By the power of the Holy Spirit, purify our conscience, so that we may forsake our sins, and put on the armor of light. Dear Lord, may we be transformed in His Holy name. Amen.

10

TENTH COMMANDMENT OF GOD.

"You shall not covet your neighbor's house; You shall not covet your neighbor's wife, nor his male servant, nor his female servant, nor his ox, nor his donkey, nor anything that is your neighbor's."

(Exodus 20:17)

"Take care and be on your guard against all covetousness, for one's life does not consist in the abundance of his possessions"

(Luke 12:15).

"What causes quarrels and what causes fights among you? Is it not this that your passions are at war within you? You desire and do not have, so you murder. You covet and cannot obtain, so you fight and quarrel"

(James 4:1-2).

In America today, quality of life is measured by the abundance of our possessions. The cliché of, "the one with the most toys wins," has become a popular bumper sticker of our times. We are always trying to get more for less, and continuously spending but never really satisfied. We are always craving something else, a faster computer, a newer car, a larger home, etc. Somehow, we never seem to be content with what we have, so we covet.

So what does it mean to covet? To covet is to crave, to really hunger after something that belongs to someone else. Coveting is strictly forbidden by the tenth commandment of God. You see, it is not that you might want something that you do not have; it is wanting something that someone else has.

If we really want a positive "change" in our country then we have to allow God to change our way of thinking, repent, and return to the Ten Commandments, which are the principles and beliefs that our Judeo/Christian society was founded on. For, coveting is in direct violation of the Judeo/Christian teaching that America was built on.

The unholy desire of coveting in man is fueled by Satan, as the god of this world (II Cor.4:4). Another way to look at coveting is wanting far more than what we would deserve or the rightful share of an individual. Instead of being envious, we should rejoice when other people are blessed by the Lord. Since coveting is the selfish approach to life, it becomes the root of our transgressions in regards to God's laws. James pointed out in the New Testament that coveting could be the root cause of many sins, including murder and warfare between nations.

In 2nd Timothy 3:1-5 we read an intensely and precise description of our world in the last days regarding coveting. It says, "But know this, that in the last days perilous times will come: For men will be lovers of themselves, lovers of money, boasters, proud, blasphemers, disobedient to parents, unthankful, unholy, unloving, unforgiving, slanderers, without self-control, brutal, despisers of good, traitors, headstrong, haughty, lovers of pleasure rather than lovers of God, having a form of godliness but denying its power. And from such people turn away"!

We see this clearly in our world today. Here in America, just look at the economy, social morality, abortion, health care, Medicare, and even social security. However, in order to begin to correct the problems in our nation's programs, we have to first "change" our hearts and allow God to change our thinking starting with the last commandment, You shall not covet.

Nine of the Ten Commandments seem to be quite practical. Do not steal, do not kill, and do not lie. All seem to be behavioral in nature. In this last commandment, God is actually introducing us to the "spiritual element" within our heart. This commandment is not behavioral; it is not concerned with what we do, in the first instance, but with what we want to do. For example, sexual gratification begins with lust. A good example is the Pro-Golfer that I mentioned briefly before, Tiger Woods. Tiger Woods is the "best" at what he does and he has the rewards to prove it. A beautiful model wife and children, his endorsements making him a millionaire many, many, times over, and everything else that follows. Nevertheless, it still was not enough for him. For Tiger Woods self-gratification came in the form of adulterous affairs. Love was not involved at all; the women were seen as a mere object of entertainment. It was, as he even admitted a feeling of "entitlement" because of what he had accomplished. Ultimately, it became a means to fulfill a sexual experience outside marriage. Yet, there are many men, of all ages, which are in the same predicament as Tiger Woods. While some men seem to say, "Why not? Tiger's got the looks, the money, go for it." The Western Media and the secularism of our nation, fuels this form of thinking, as it continues to become increasingly hostile to the Judeo-Christian values. Even in our public schools, we see a demand of "value neutrality" as compromise in the teaching of morality to students. We are living in an age where adolescent sexual activity is normal, so why not give out condoms. Sin is being downplayed and morality is being compromised. You see, this is why covetousness is such a dangerous thing. It is seldom content in remaining closed in the heart of man; it always has a way of poisoning the lives of many, until the only thing that matters is getting what it wants, regardless of the price that society has to pay. Then, the funny thing is that it never ends, there is always more to want, or there is never enough.

I read of one of the legends to originate out of the history of rock and roll music, the lead guitarist of the Rolling Stones, Keith Richards. According to the story, one night after a long bout with drugs, sex, and alcohol, Keith Richards fell into a drug-induced sleep. Then during the early morning hours, he awoke with a series of musical notes in his head. Even though he said that he had no memory of this, he got up and wrote down the music that was on his head. When he sobered up and saw the music that he had written, he began to play it on his guitar, and it was perhaps the most famous song in rock and roll music, as it became the smash hit for the Rolling Stones, "I Can't Get No Satisfaction." Many people cannot be satisfied regardless of what they posses. In Luke 12:19 we read, "Soul, you have many goods laid up for many years, take your ease; eat, drink and be merry." Nevertheless, the man in this story did not please God, who plainly disliked his callous, selfish attitude and love for the material world. Humanity has long been afflicted by the curse of covetousness. As James pointed out in James: 14-15, coveting can be the root cause of many of our sins. Serious sins such as murder and even warfare. You see, it is explained that what begins as a thought becomes an obsession that will ultimately lead to the sinful act. Let's face it, how many times have we let our desires rule the way we think and act? The desires of the flesh are uninhibited pleasures, unrestrained desires, and unsuppressed passion for things of the world. Again, unless we make a promise to ourselves, to keep covetousness under control, it will control you.

Coveting is a modern problem that is really the curse of our humanity. Common outcome of this day and age, are the millions of people that are drowning in debt. They bought the items that they lusted for but could not really afford, on their credit card. I remember going to see a hospice patient at his home, early in my career. I was impressed by the guarded gate, the awesome landscaping, the fountains, the lakes, and of course the homes in the community. My patient's home was no less impressive with Spanish marble throughout the house and an amazing view of the lake out of his large bedroom window. Unfortunately, many of the stylish furniture items were being repossessed and the home was facing foreclosure. A bad economy, illness, and a large amount of credit debt made it impossible to maintain his luxurious life style. He told me that he did not plan to get sick, and hoped to have paid it all back. He agreed that he liked the "better things in life" and might have over spent his income. However, for me what came to mind were the principles expressed by Paul in the Bible. He said, "For we brought nothing into this world, and it is certain that we can carry nothing out. Having food and clothing, which these shall we be content. Nevertheless, those who desire to be rich fall into temptation and a snare, and into many foolish and harmful lusts, which drown men in destruction and perdition. For the love of money is the root of all kinds of evil, for which some have strayed from the faith in their greediness, and pierced themselves through with many sorrows" (1Timothy 6:7-10).

Psychologists say that when "things" are obtained, there is usually a rush or a feeling of fulfillment for the person. Many times people seek that feeling and become addicted to buying. It does make them happy, but only temporarily. Man's tendency to covet only leads to idolize the material world as the only sense of contentment in life. As Keith Richard's famous words say, "I can't get no satisfaction". When are we going to learn that God's instructions are timeless?

In the Bible, we are told regarding the last days, that many in the end time will be "lovers of themselves, lovers of money," (2 Timothy 3:2). I personally believe that covetousness combined with greed is the major cause of the economic mess that America is currently experiencing. You see, covetousness among men is a powerful drug that corrupts their judgment. The mentality of "what is in it for me?" makes a weak soul subject to bribes and can destroy a person's integrity.

Friends, we need to adjust our desires in the direction that Jesus commanded us to follow. Jesus explained that we should "seek first the kingdom of God and His righteousness" (Mathew 6:33). Remember that Jesus also instructed us to "Lay up for yourselves treasures in heaven, where neither moth nor rust destroys and where thieves do not break in and steal. For where your treasure is, there your heart will also be" (Mathew 6:20-21).

So what are the lasting treasures that God is referring to? Personal and fulfilling associations with family and friends, spiritual discernment, life's work that glorifies God, maintaining a path of righteousness, and most importantly, to purify our hearts so that it can become a temple for the Lord. Remember, the Lord Jesus Christ promises great rewards for those who have managed to maintain a pure heart. "Blessed are the pure in heart for they shall see God" (Mathew 5:8). Paul made it very clear when he said, "Do you not know that you are the temple of God and that the Spirit of God dwells in you? If anyone defiles the temple of God, God will destroy him. For the temple of God is holy, and you are that temple" (1Cor. 3:16-17). Those are some of the examples of the lasting treasures that Jesus was referring to in His gospel. Jesus has promised us an eternal and blessed life in the Kingdom of Heaven, filled with His infinite love. So, why not pile up those "lasting treasures" of Christ here on earth, to enjoy an amazing eternal life.

When a young Jewish boy asked Jesus what he should do in order to inherit everlasting life, the Lord, Jesus replied, "Observe the commandments." Then He enumerated several commandments from the list of ten (Mathew 19: 16-22). In so many of His sermons, the Lord, Jesus repeated the importance of the Ten Commandments of God. In all those times, Jesus took the time to completely explain their spiritual and religious meaning. Jesus knew that the Ten Commandments gave humanity the fundamental moral guidance needed for society to function properly, within the limits of reason.

Today more than ever, America needs the Ten Commandments. America also needs courageous men and women willing to stand and uphold the Laws of God, and preach the Gospel of Jesus Christ to a lost and hurting world. We live in a world searching for answers. Remember that Jesus took His message of hope into the streets, telling those without God in their life, that there is a better way to live. In God's Love and Care.

God has called us to take His message, the message of the Love of Jesus Christ to a world that rejects any aspects of God. Remember that the God of Israel did not call us to hide under a bushel, but to share His light with this dark world that we live in. Furthermore, there is no need to be afraid of spreading the love and hope of Jesus Christ to a dying world because like 1 John 4:4

tells us, "Greater is He that is in you than he that is in the world". Now is the time to be the salt and the light of the world, it is time to bodily present the message of Truth to those directly opposed to His commandments.

America, unfortunately, has plunged into unrestrained immorality, corruption, and rejection of Godly values. This has not gone unnoticed by our Lord. Today, the vast majority of people seem to follow the path of self-determination, introduced to humanity in Genesis 3 by Adam and Eve. This would be classified by society's immoral emphasis on personal pleasure, at any cost, over respect for life and biblical teaching. Friends, let me close with words to ponder and a prayer, as we pray to God to give us courage to remain true to God and to our beliefs of morality.

Words to Contemplate: Paradox of Time.

In our modern world we spend more, but seem to have less.
We buy more but have less time to enjoy it.
We have bigger houses but much smaller families.
We have more conveniences but have less time.
We have more degrees, yet we have less sense.
We have more knowledge, but less judgment.
We have more experts, but less solutions.
We have more medicine, but less health.
We have multiplied our possessions, but have reduced our values.
We talk too much, love too little, and hate too often.
We have learned how to make a living, but not a life.
We have added years to life, but not life to the years.
We have been all the way to the moon and back, but we have trouble crossing the street to meet our neighbor.
We have conquered outer space, but not our inner soul.
We have higher incomes, but lower morale.
These are the times of world peace but domestic violence.
These are the days of two income families but more divorce. Of fancier houses, but broken homes.
Yes, these are the times of tall men with short character in office.
Rev. Bob Moorhead.

Let us pray:

All Powerful God of Mercy, we bless You in the name of your beloved Son, Jesus Christ. Look with tolerance and kindness on the United States of America. Deliver us from sin and incline the hearts of this nation to keep Your Ten Commandments, so that all hearts and minds will be set on doing Your holy will. With confidence, may we will remain strong against any assaults from our enemies and fearlessly stand tall against all forms of evil. Grant, dear Lord, that the guidance of the Holy Spirit be forever present in our nation, as it will always remain, "One Nation Under God".

Praise be to You, Lord Jesus Christ. Amen.

11

FUTURE OF GOD IN AMERICA

Our United States of America has been highly distinguished around the world as a Christian Nation, a nation that offers freedom and opportunity for people from all lifestyles. Millions and millions of people have come to America, from all parts of the world to experience for themselves the "land of the free". The Statue of Liberty has a famous inscription which reads, "Give me your tired, your poor, your huddled masses yearning to be free, the wretched refuse of tempest-tossed to me. I lift my lamp beside the golden door." Yes, America has had a long legacy of compassion, charity, and generosity. America, the light of the world, always sacrificing, even the lives of our men, to assist the needy and protect the oppressed around the globe.

Unfortunately, America has recently plunged into a sea of uncontrolled immorality, as the rejection of Godly values, the Ten Commandments, becomes a way of life. Ultimately, expelling God from all aspects of public life or the public square. We are living in very serious times, we need to wake up individually and nationally, or prepare for the worst devastation in the history of this nation. You see friends; it is because of our disobedience and defiance towards Almighty God that our nation has lost favor with Him. Throughout the history of our nation, God has been quite gracious, bestowing blessings of all kinds to His favored land, America. However, that has slowly but surely come to a complete halt. Allow me to summarize when we began to lose our grace with God and where we are now.

Going back to the early 1960's, respect for God in America began to fade. This event began to happen "against" the opinion of the majority of the American population. The Supreme Court of America, declared prayer in public school system unconstitutional, the Ten Commandments removed from public properties, and women were given the right have abortions on demand. The American way of life started slowly moving further and further from God's way of life. America started to become defiant in the face of her Creator.

The American Civil Liberties Union (ACLU) also took up their cause with a passion; unfortunately, their passion was not favoring God in the court system. As they started representing various atheists individuals and atheists groups, the ACLU became quite successful in removing Christmas decorations from public land and buildings around the nation. They removed Christmas plays and Christmas carols, and just recently, they were "victorious" in removing the opening prayer at public schools sporting events and graduation ceremonies. Unfortunately, corporate America, fearful of legal actions, from groups such as the ACLU, has complied with their demands and now observes a **"politically correct policy."** Under this policy, it is forbidden to use words such as God, Lord, Jesus Christ, or even Merry Christmas in public. Atheists want all signs of God to be erased from public eyes, and with the assistance of the ACLU, they are having success in removing everything that might be considered Christian in nature. For example, the ACLU in 2001, on behalf of a retired park employee, sued the Mojave National Preserve because it had a cross, sitting on federal land. The federal courts sided with the ACLU and ordered the cross to be taken down. However, the cross has an amazing history, the Veterans of Foreign Wars erected the cross back in 1934. It was erected in memory of the soldiers who fought and died in World War I. The cross was even designated as a war memorial by Congress and has served as the site of the yearly Easter sunrise service. I am proud to state that at the printing of this book, six Supreme Court justices rejected the order to remove the WWI memorial from the federal preserve. God does respond to the prayers of His faithful people.

The Ten Commandments are also under attack and we have seen evidence of this as they have been removed from public buildings across our nation. Currently, public outcry and a recent court ruling have prevented their attempts to remove "IN GOD WE TRUST" from our currency. The Pledge of Allegiance has also been under assault, as a campaign was launched to remove the "under God" portion. Although, so far, such attempts have failed, only God knows how much longer there will be any public references to Him.

It is a fact that Christians in America still make up the largest percentage of the American population. However, they have remained a silent majority, unknowing, or unwilling to stand up for the God of the Bible who is being severely attacked in America today. Unless Americans watch the *Fox News Channel* or spend time going to web sites of organizations dedicated to the defense and promotion of the religious freedoms in America, they are simply unaware of the spiritual battle going on in our country right now. Are you spiritually brave? Are you willing to take a stand for God?

As I mentioned earlier, the Ten Commandments were rules for life given by God to the people of Israel on Mount Sinai. The commandments were written on two stone tablets, unfortunately, they are being shattered everyday here in America. The politically correct policies and the separation of church and state have replaced them. The ACLU has used the separation of church and state rulings to their advantage and has transformed America, once a Christian nation to a secular one. By representing and winning many rulings for the non-believers, some from other nations, they have replaced the belief that the majority rules. I wonder what would happen if an ACLU attorney went to an Islamic nation and represented Christian rights?

Our founding fathers did not want religionist fanatics in charge of their new nation, but they did pray to God for guidance and wisdom. So they drafted up a document called the "Constitution" which insured the freedom of its citizens by having three separate branches of government, The Executive, the Legislative, and the

Judicial. All of the three branches are subjected to the rule that the majority of votes prevails. However, now we are seeing evidence of the rights of the minority winning over the rights of the majority. When did we lose perspective as a nation?

Fifty years ago when the Supreme Court ruled that prayer in the public schools was unconstitutional, the law of "separation of church and state" became the law of modern and secular America. The ACLU and other similar organizations, using this court decision started the eradication of biblical teachings and religious holiday practices from public schools, government agencies, non-profit organizations, and even private corporations. Thus, if your child is currently attending public school, he/she is learning in an atheist environment, where teachers are instructed to teach and explain man's existence based on Darwin's evolutionary theory. Fearful of losing their jobs, fined, or even imprisoned, teachers will not lecture on the theory of Intelligent Design. I thought that the purpose of an education was to allow young minds to examine the different aspects of a subject matter.

The assault on biblical teaching of the Ten Commandments continues today, but before I discuss a few recent cases, I would like to bring to mind an older case dealing with the removing of the Ten Commandments monument from a judicial building. Alabama Chief Justice Roy Moore made national news when he refused to remove the monument that was ordered by U. S. District Judge Myron Thompson to be done. Judge Thompson ruled that it violated the principle of separation of church and state. The outcome was the removal of Justice Roy Moore from his position and he being charged with ethics violations. Polls at that time showed only 25% of Americans approved of the court order to remove the Ten Commandments. Can you see how the opinions of a few in authorities can nullify the opinion of the majority?

The ACLU claims to be dedicated to protecting the freedom of all Americans. Unfortunately, it has a history of defending abortionists, pornographers, and child molesters. Nonetheless, when it comes to attacking the Judeo/Christian value system of America, the ACLU is ruthless. The ACLU constant attack on God will not stop until

God is detached from our shores. Impossible you say! Yes, it is true that current court rulings have slowed the march to make America an atheist nation, but regrettably the majority of our present political leaders are very liberal minded. They no longer hear the voice of the Christian. Will Obama care allow abortions to be the new form of birth control, since congress has the power to remove the Hyde Amendment?

The ACLU has filed lawsuits throughout the United States to remove the Ten Commandments and the Christian crosses from public buildings and land. Federal, state, and local government agencies have removed these symbols voluntarily to avoid lawsuits that can become extremely expensive to fight. A few have held their ground, true to what they believe in, religious freedom in America. How many people do you think will come to their aid financially?

As I mentioned before, the cross in the Mojave Desert caused quite a bit of controversy. Although the ACLU filed a lawsuit to have it removed and the court agreed, public prayer and protest from American citizens, veterans groups, and congressional efforts have been able to save the cross once again. So what is next, removing crosses at national cemeteries? Let us look at the future. If a citizen is upset at seeing a religious symbols on a private buildings, could he/she get ordinances passed to ban them on new construction?

On March of 2010, Stigler, Oklahoma had to remove a monument of the Ten Commandments from its county courthouse lawn. The Supreme Court had decided not to hear the case, and this allowed the ruling of the federal judge to stand. Around the same time, the state of Texas, decided to ask its voters for their opinion on God and government. Over 95% of the voters believed that the word God and the Ten Commandments should be allowed in the public square. Can you see how the majority vote is not being represented in the courts?

A math teacher from San Diego, California was ordered by the California School Board to remove the patriotic banners from the walls of the classrooms because it may reference to "God." Teacher Bradley Johnson with the help of the Thomas Moore Law Center won this suit in the Federal District Court.

The banners that the California School Board wanted removed had phrases such as "God Bless America," "In God We Trust," and "One Nation Under God". Currently they are appealing the ruling. The school board's position is that the banners are advocating a non-permissible Judeo/Christian view and may be offensive to Muslim students. Does not our currency and pledge allegiance to the flag have the same wording?

Atheist Michael Newdow with 59 other atheist activists got together at the White House with members of the Obama Administration on February 26, 2010. This group believes that God has no place in America. The vast majority of people, from all faiths should be outraged by this event. I wonder if they asked the president to stop saying, "God bless America" at the end of his speeches.

Finally God Wins! On March 12, 2010 Michael Newdow, the recent White House visitor, lost his suit in the ninth U. S. Circuit Court of Appeals. The Court rejected his two legal challenges that the words "Under God" in the Pledge of Allegiance and "In God We Trust" on the U.S. currency violate the separation of church and state. In a 2-1 court panel ruling, Judge Carlos Bea determined that these phrases are constitutional. However, God won by only one vote. How will the liberal judges rule in 50 years? Please remember who is selecting new Federal and Supreme Court justices today in America, President Obama!

Currently, some wonderful law centers that stand for God and justice in our nation. Here are a few that assisted me against the hospice that denied me the right to use God in my organizational prayers. Please visit the websites of Liberty Counsel, Thomas Moore Law Center, Alliance Defense Fund, and the American Center for Law and Justice to learn more. These spiritual warriors need our donations to fight the immorality that is taking over this great nation.

As secularism continues to grow and becomes more accepted, we see a very different America from the one of days past. Science has replaced God in schools, metal detectors and armed police in high schools have replaced Morning Prayer and the viewing of the Ten Commandments. When the children return home from school, they return to a house lacking in adult supervision and loving care. Most teenagers now days eat dinner watching television or using the computer or on their cell phones. All these events occur away from their family members. After dinner, it is guaranteed that they will return to the same types of activities. These electrical marvels have essentially replaced time with God and family. As the American liberal media continues to change American values, we see that love and commitment to God and others have been replaced by materialism, casual drug use and sexual pleasures without love just to name a few. Will these children know God personally?

Now, let us look at America's 44th President, Mr. Barack Hussein Obama. He comes from a divorced middle class family, he is bi-racial, he is highly intelligent, well educated, well liked, respected by many, and has achieved remarkable success in his young life. He holds the highest office in the land as President of the United States of America. However, his ideas on how to transform America are very secular in nature, and he is experiencing resistance from many people who have placed their allegiance in God and country. Mr. Obama claims to be a Christian; however, his beliefs seem to be in conflict with God's laws, specifically, the Ten Commandments. His value system contradicts that of a Godly way of life.

As we look at President Obama's accomplishments during his short time in office, it almost seems as though he is waging a campaign against Christianity and our Christian tradition, which for many Americans has been the foundation of this country. Consider first what President Obama said on June 2007. "Whatever we once were, we are no longer a Christian nation, at least, not just. We are also a Jewish nation, a Muslim nation, a Buddhist nation and a Hindu nation, and a nation of nonbelievers". President Obama; why must you dishonor the Biblical roots of American history? Do you feel that it is our belief in a Christian God that causes Islamic religious extremists to hate us? No Mr. Obama, we are hated due to the envy they have for us, western oppression, foreign policies, and a society gone Godless. We must remember that the Ten Commandments of God are also in the Koran.

In a recent trip to Turkey, President Obama again gave his anti-

Christian message, "One of the great strengths of the United States of America is that it does not consider itself a Christian nation or a Jewish nation, or a Muslim nation. We consider ourselves a nation of citizens who are bound by ideals and a set of values" (CNN Report). "Well, Mr. President you have it all wrong. You see the great strength of America is derived from the fact that we are, and have always been a Christian nation." "And, as Christians we are tolerant of all faith traditions." "Did you know Mr. President that in a study conducted by the 2008 American Religious Identification Survey, 76% of the population identify themselves as Christian?"

However, President Obama continues to verbalize the non-Christian agenda overseas. He specifies that his sets of principles be identified by a promise of a secular country that is respectful of religious freedom, respectful of the rule of law, and respectful of personal freedom. His value system is to have a commonly agreed morality that forbids any display of faith in the public square. However, that demands for a completely secular country, forbidding or rejecting the existing belief system that this country was founded on. In such a design for this country, there is no room for the Ten Commandments or for that matter, God. Therefore, welcome to the "New Atheist Nation."

Remember the invitation for President Obama to speak at the Jesuit University, Georgetown, in April of 2009. Mr. Obama and his White House team made some outrageous demands of the catholic university, and the sad irony of it is that the university complied with their demands. All visible signs and symbols of Jesus Christ were asked to be covered up including the **IHS** monogram. Many people in the general population do not even know that this monogram symbolizes the name of Jesus Christ.

This Catholic University must have forgotten a letter from Paul to Timothy, "If we deny Him, He will also deny us."

Continuing with the President's accomplishments, we see that only 4 days into office the President reversed the Mexico City Policy. This states that instead of restricting foreign aid to organizations that directly support abortions, we, the American taxpayers, will now be funding abortions overseas. In addition, President Obama nominated the most pro-abortion governor in the country, Kansas Governor Kathleen Sebelius, to be Secretary of HHS, which oversees millions of dollars spent on the abortion industry. President Obama also has started the proceedings to eliminate the "conscience clause" which were regulations that were put in place by President Bush. These regulations protected the healthcare professionals who refused to perform abortions for moral reasons. Sadly, under President Obama's health care plan, the same supporters for taxpayer-funded abortions are also the ones advocating wiping out parental consent laws for minor to obtain abortions.

What about research, with stem cells that are obtained from aborted fetuses? President Obama has signed an executive order that forces the American taxpayer to fund unrestricted embryonic stem cell research. Therefore, the culture of death, of Mr. Obama continues. What happened to "Thou shall not kill"?

However, currently many are praising President Obama for his deep commitment and appreciation of the Muslim faith. Here is some of his statements in context, which he made to the Turkish parliament.

"I also want to be clear that America's relationship with the Muslim community, the Muslim world, cannot and will not, just be based upon opposition to terrorism. We seek a broader engagement based on mutual interest and mutual respect. We will listen carefully, we will bridge misunderstandings, and we will seek common ground. We will convey our deep appreciation for the Islamic faith, which has done so much over the centuries to shape the world—including our own country. Muslim Americans have enriched the United States. Many other Americans have Muslims in their families or have lived in a Muslim majority country---I know because I am one of them."

What the President of the United States does not seem to realize is that America and the Islam nations offer two very different and fundamentally irreconcilable visions of society. For America, our Constitution and many of its laws were derived from knowledge obtained by our founding fathers from the Holy Bible. The Judeo/Christian faith traditions birthed America, and these biblical beliefs became the rock that American freedoms where curved on. As for the Muslim world, it is to work and pray that humankind submits to the Koran. Many Muslims see this as their lifetime goal, and their solemn pledge to Allah. However, for me, and for many American Christians, the primary concern of these differences is strictly theological and spiritual. Christian Americans believe that Jesus Christ is the Messiah, the Word that became Flesh, God Incarnate, He is God. Jesus was not "just" a prophet, as the Muslim population believes. This includes our President, whose statements over-seas places Jesus and Mohammed on same level of importance. Jesus Christ is God, is a concept that the Muslim world will never accept. We as American Christians will never deny that indeed, Jesus is God and Savior.

A collogue of mine once said, "around the world many have concerns that the United States of America is to be understood and acknowledged as a Christian nation, however, in the same manner, the nations of Islam want to be understood and acknowledged as Muslims. So if this is the case, then unfortunately, Islam will continue to be at war with America." The Koran is not open for discussion or interpretation, for it is considered the word of Allah. This word comes with orders and requests that need to be fulfilled regardless of place or time. As the Turkish Prime Minister Erdogan once said, "There is no moderate Islam, Islam is Islam."

Now let us look at the First Amendment of the constitution of the United States. Many in America perceive it as "separation of church and state," and yet that is completely erroneous. The exact language is as follows: "Congress shall make no law respecting the establishment of religion, or prohibiting the free exercise thereof...." As a nation, we have adhered to a rule, "separation of church and state," and yet that law does not exist. The First Amendment defines, "Freedom of Religion, not freedom from religion, and the "Right of Free Speech, and the Right of Free Press." It also includes the "Right of Assembly and Petition."

The Supreme Court used the following letter from Thomas Jefferson to the Danbury Baptists for its decision that the **separation of church and state** should be the law of the land. *"Believing with* *you that religion is a matter which lies solely between man and his God, that he owes account to none other for his faith or his worship, that the legitimate powers of government reach actions only and not opinions, I contemplate with sovereign reverence that act of the whole American people which declared that their legislature should make no law respecting an establishment of religion, or prohibiting the free exercise thereof, thus* building a wall of separation between church and state".

Thomas Jefferson was a very spiritual person, who prayed to God daily. I do not think he would approve of the court rulings that a generic prayer to God and the Ten Commandants be unconstitutional, and removed from public life. Atheists and people of little faith have convinced Americans that our founding fathers wanted a complete separation of church and state. This is false; one only needs to study the lives of our founders to gain knowledge of this fact.

Just as our founding fathers relied on the guidance and care from God to create the greatest country in the world, we, as Americans, cannot allow the God of the Holy Bible to be evicted from our way of life. The new humanistic and secular approach that we are witnessing in our government today is in fact, mandating the new religion of "Atheism" to flourish in America. God's undeniable influence in our country's history has been downplayed long enough, and it is now being eradicated from our daily lives. We must not allow a vocal minority to strip away every reference to God in our society. Public prayer and open discussions about Jesus Christ or His Word are coming under attack daily and it is outright prohibition in the public square.

There is a solution to this problem in America. It is the revival of dependence on God and His Ten Commandments. In order for the Ten Commandments to guide us and help our nation, we must make them our own. The Ten Commandments should become our viewpoint and our guide. They should permeate our subconscious. King David wrote: "Blessed is the man who walks not in the counsel of the ungodly, nor stands in the oath of sinners, nor sits in the seat of the scornful; but his delight is in the law of the Lord, and in His law he meditates day and night. He shall be like a tree planted by the rivers of water that brings forth its fruit in its season, whose leaf also shall not wither and whatever he does shall prosper" (Psalm 1:1-3).

Friends, we must abide by the Ten Commandments, it is our only saving grace. Unfortunately, millions of modern Christians embrace the popular line, "Christianity is not about actual obedience to the Ten Commandments, but whether or not you love Jesus and have a relationship with Him." May I remind you of what Jesus said, "And why do you call me Lord, Lord, and do not do the things which I say" (Luke 6:46)?

If God asked me to analyze my findings, and to provide Him with a picture on how He stands in America today and in years to come, my response would be as follows: "God, You will be pleased to know that today in America there are many people that worship and glorify You. However, many of them are graying and will be with You soon in heaven". We were taught as children that America has always enjoyed Your blessings. Yet today many of our leaders do not call You Lord, even though they end their speeches with "God Bless America." Unfortunately, I am sorry to report that Your Name can no longer be said in our public schools. Your laws, the Ten Commandments, cannot be displayed on public land. The phrases, separation of church and state, and being politically correct are now the law of our land."

"Americans of the 21ˢᵗ century are very busy, and their lifestyles do not include daily time for You. Both husband and wife are working hard to pay for the house, the cars, and the vacations. The little free time available to them is utilized using the computer, shopping, entertainment, sporting events, or simply paying the bills. Since time for You does not exist in modern America, our children will not be introduced to You like in years past. Your teachings will not be emphasized. Satan's laws, (separation of church and state, and being politically correct) and the lack of time will turn millions of people lukewarm or away from You. God, You will be replaced with a secular and humanistic way of life which has the belief that You do not exist. It is a new religion called "Atheism." A vocal minority which claims that if we refer to You, we are promoting Christianity.

Under this pretense, the minority defies the Constitution of the United States by stating that those who believe in You are making life difficult for those who don't.

"Lord, we know that You extend to us Your loving act of undeserved mercy, compassion, deliverance and pardon for our offenses against You. In both, Exodus 20:2 and Deuteronomy 5:6, Lord, You demonstrate Your grace by beginning with the following statement: "I am the Lord your God who brought you out of the land of Egypt, and out of the house of bondage". You have built Your grace into Your Ten Commandments. In the Gospel of Jesus Christ, again You remind us of Your love for us, "But God demonstrate His own love toward us, in that while we were still sinners, Christ died for us" (Romans 5:8). Jesus Christ made the ultimate sacrifice to prove God's love for us, long before we were even capable of returning that love back to Him. So my friends, there is always hope with God.

Finally, I would like to mention once again that this book is dedicated to God, Creator of Heaven and Earth, and to Jesus Christ, His only Son and Savior. This book was composed without any thought of personal gain. The content of this book is not new. Many articles, books, and movies have tried before to alert the American public that unless action is taken, America will become a socialistic and Godless society.

A good example is Ben Stein's documentary. *Expelled: No Intelligence Allowed:* Mr. Stein exposes the evils and dangers of presenting only one side of the argument of creation. The movie revealed to its viewers that college and university professors, who were advocates of the intelligent design theory, became victims of religious discrimination by the scientific community. Both, the scientific community and atheists groups criticized Mr. Stein's work. So do not count on seeing this movie on any major TV network; however, it is available at video stores.

I pray to the Lord, our God, that He will bless this book. That it will open the eyes of millions of Americans who abide by the laws of God, to see how our Lord is being "Expelled" from America today and what can be done to prevent it. Know, my friends, that world events do not catch God by surprise. He is placing each one of us precisely where He wants us for a purpose. Do not allow your surroundings to determine how you live your life. Let God use you to make a difference in this generation. The silent majority must act now with our voice, prayers, <u>votes</u>, and talents to change America's path to atheism. Together as brothers and sisters, with one strong voice, we can keep God in America for our future generations. May God bless all of us in this battle to keep God alive in the hearts of all humanity.

APPENDIX

National Day of Prayer

Ruled Unconstitutional

On April 15, 2010, US District Judge Crabb ruled that the National Day of Prayer violated the First Amendment's prohibition on government endorsement of religion. She like many of the federal judges before her must had slept through American History. The majority of our founding fathers had a strong belief in a 'Creator' and prayed for His wisdom and guidance.

Prayer was said at the beginning of the Continental Congress meetings, Thomas Jefferson founded churches, and the US government printed bibles. Most of the founding fathers made statements to the importance of a belief in God and His Ten Commandments, for the freedoms that America enjoys.

Judge Crabb, is the US military forcing people to participate in this day of prayer? NO! Congress first authorized the National Day of Prayer in 1952. At that time, it was the will of the people to honor the first commandment of God, ***I am the Lord thy God.*** Since this is the same belief as our founding fathers, your ruling must be causing them to turn over in their graves.

If allowed to stay, will this ruling open the door to make Easter Egg Hunts unconstitutional on public land? Will Christmas be removed as one of our national holiday? Americans if you stay quiet, your grandchildren and great grandchildren will live in an atheistic and socialistic nation. The choice is yours.

America's Moral Decline

Americans report widespread acceptance of indulging in many behaviors that are considered immoral by biblical teachings and conflicts with God's Ten Commandments

Behavior	Percentage of Accepting
Gambling	61
Cohabitation	+60
Sexual fantasizing	59
Abortion	+45
Adultery	+42
Pornography	+38
Profanity	+36
Drunkenness	35
Homosexual Sex	+30
Use of non-prescription drugs	+17

Source: Morality Continues to Decay: Barna Study, Nov. 2003

+Independent new Surveys show increases in these numbers as more Americans deny God.

Interesting Statistics about Church and God in America

3500-4000 churches close their doors each year. (From the Barna Study)

Only 21% of Americans attend religious services weekly. (www.religioustolerence.org)

Those claiming to be Christian declined from 91% in 1948 to 75% in 2009. (Trinity College Study)

Those claiming to be non-Christian religious groups increased from about 5.6 million to about 7.7 million. (American Religious identification Survey)

Religious make up the United States (2005-Wikipedia.org)

Protestant (51.3%)   Roman Catholic (23.9%)

Mormon (1.7%)   Other Christian (1.6%)

Unaffiliated (12.1)

Other or unspecified (2.5%)

Buddhist (0.7%)

Muslim (0.6%) (Only religion not declining in U.S.)

People who do not attend church are more likely to feel stressed out; less optimistic; less concerned about moral condition of the nation; and are less likely to believe they are making a positive difference in the world. (Barna Study)

Research shows that people who attend church live longer. (www. washingtontimes.com)

A recent Harris Poll found that 82% of American believes in God. However, when asked how certain they were, only 59% are "absolutely certain" that there is a God, and another 15% say they are somewhat certain.

According to a 2006 survey, 52% of American says they believe that the Bible is God's **authorities' word. But only 36% believe people should live by God's principles; 15% say they will** live by their own principles even if they conflict with God's principles; and 45% prefer to combine God's teaching and their own values.

THE LATE PRESIDENT RONALD REAGAN STATEMENT ON GOD AND COUNTRY

(Did he foresee America's Future?)

Our Pledge of Allegiance states that we are "one nation under God," and our currency bears the motto "In God We Trust." The morality and values such faith implies are deeply embedded in our national character. Our country embraces those principles by design, and we abandon them at our peril. Yet in recent years... America... (have) for the sake of religious tolerance... Forbidden religious practice in the classroom. The law of this land has effectively removed prayer from our classrooms. How can we hope to retain freedom through the generations if we fail to teach our young that our liberty springs from an abiding faith in our Creator?

James Madison

Known as the Father of the Constitution and the fourth President of the United States, James Madison made the following statement; "We have staked the whole future of the American Civilization... upon the capacity of each and all of us to govern ourselves according to the Ten Commandments of God."

PRAYER FOR AMERICA.

God of liberty, America acknowledges Your reign.
For the freedom of our land.

For the rights that we possess.

For the security of our laws.

We praise Your Name.

Give guidance to our leaders.

Watch over those who serve their country well.

Raise up the poor and exalt the meek and humble.

Never let us be separated from Your care.

Make our nation great and strong again.

Make Your love the foundation of our land.

Renowned in wisdom, prosperous in virtues, and renewed in faith.

May Your Word be allowed in the public square. For all to see and hear.

May Your Ten Commandments be followed and revered.

Father, America sheds its tears for a land that was loved and lost. We have journeyed through dark valleys, but Your light will lead us to a place of love and hope.

America is determined and resolved to do what is good and right.

To destroy all signs of division and to live by Your light.

Father, fill us with Your peace and keep us in Your presence. Anoint us with Your motivation and inspire us to stand tall. America, we are one people, united in praising the One Holy God.

With courage and honor our nation will stand.

To protect our freedom and the God of our land.

Amen.

Rev. Mirta Signorelli.

Relevant Biblical Verses

I urge you, first of all, to pray for all people. Ask God to help them; intercede on their behalf, and give thanks for them. Pray this way for kings and all who are in authority so that we can live peaceful and quiet lives marked by godliness and dignity. This is good and pleases God our Savior, who wants everyone to be saved and to understand the truth

(1Timothy 2:1-4).

All men will hate you because of me, but he who stands firm to the end will be saved

(Matthew 10:22).

Be sober, be vigilant; because your adversary the devil, as a roaring lion, walketh about, seeking whom he may devour

(1 Peter 5:8).

If my people, who are called by my name, will humble themselves and pray and seek my face and turn from their wicked ways, then will I hear from heaven and will forgive their sin and will heal their land

(2Chronicles 7:14).

He who is not with Me is against Me; and he who does not gather with Me scatters

(Matthew 6:24).

TUESDAY, MARCH 17, 2009

This story, which turned out to be one of the last I wrote for the Sun Sentinel, caused a great sensation. It went out on the Internet and whipped around the world, quickly attracting 175,000 hits and getting lots of play on, you guessed it, Fox News. I wrote it as straight-down-the-middle news story. But the reason it got so much attention is the absurdity of the hospice position: so afraid of offense, it reduces a chaplain's message to pabulum.

CHAPLAIN RESIGNS OVER RULE AT HOSPICE
Sun-Sentinel

By Howard Goodman
Sun Sentinel Staff Writer

A chaplain at Hospice by the Sea in Boca Raton has resigned, she says, over a ban on use of the words "God" or "Lord" in public settings.

Chaplains still speak freely of the Almighty in private sessions with patients or families, but the Rev. Mirta Signorelli said: "I can't do chaplain's work if I can't say 'God' - if I'm scripted."

Hospice CEO Paula Alderson said the ban on religious references applies only to the inspirational messages that chaplains deliver in staff meetings. The hospice remains fully comfortable with ministers, priests, and rabbis offering religious counsel to the dying and grieving.

"I was sensitive to the fact that we don't impose religion on our staff, and that it is not appropriate in the context of a staff meeting to use certain phrases or 'God' or 'Holy Father,' because some of our staff don't believe at all," Alderson said.

Signorelli, of Royal Palm Beach, said the hospice policy has a chilling effect that goes beyond the monthly staff meetings. She would have to watch her language, she said, when leading a prayer in the hospice chapel, when meeting patients in the public setting of a nursing home and in weekly patient conferences with doctors, nurses and social workers.

"If you take God away from me," she said, "it's like taking a medical tool away from a nurse."

A devout Christian who acquired a master's degree in theology after a career as a psychologist, running a program for abused and neglected children, Signorelli has been ministering to the dying for 13 years. She worked at the Hospice of Palm Beach County before moving seven years ago to Hospice by the Sea, a community-based nonprofit organization that cares for terminally ill patients in Palm Beach and Broward counties.

Signorelli said that she and other chaplains were told Feb. 23 to "cease and desist from using God in prayers."

Signorelli said her supervisor recently singled her out for delivering a spiritual reflection in the chapel that included the word "Lord" and had "a Christian connotation."

"But that was the 23rd Psalm," Signorelli said - not, strictly speaking, Christian, as it appears in the Old Testament.

"And I am well aware that there were people from the Jewish tradition in attendance. I didn't say Jesus or Allah or Jehovah. I used 'Lord' and 'God,' which I think are politically correct. I think that's as generic as you can get."

Signorelli resigned Feb. 25.

None of the six other chaplains objected to the ban on God's name, she said.

Alderson said she was surprised by Signorelli's reaction to what she characterized as a minor administrative directive aimed solely at improving the decorum of monthly staff meetings, where the desired tone from a chaplain should be motivational, not religious.

Alderson said it started after she asked a chaplain - not Signorelli - to say something "inspirational" and "thought-provoking" at a staff meeting. The remarks did not strike the secular tone she wanted, Alderson said. So, "I issued some guidelines."

Guidelines from HealthCare Chaplaincy, a multi-faith organization, state that professional chaplains should "reach across faith group boundaries and not proselytize." But they don't tell chaplains to refrain from speaking about God

.

I hope this is some sort of misunderstanding," said Rita Kaufman, spokeswoman for the Association of Professional Chaplains, based in Schaumburg, Ill.

Hospice of Palm Beach County has not barred "God," marketing director Karen Stearns said. It does direct chaplains to be sensitive to patients' religious sensibilities.

Likewise, a ban on the word "God" was new to Mathew Staver, founder and chairman of Liberty Counsel, a religious-freedom organization based in Orlando.

"That seems quite bizarre, and a significant restriction on her freedom of speech," Staver said.

Noting that spirituality has been linked to mortality and morbidity rates, Staver added: "To excise God from someone who is a grief counselor seems to be an extreme and uncalled-for response."

Hospice by the Sea, founded in 1979, provides services to about 500 patients every day on an annual budget of $35 million. Most revenue comes from Medicare, Medicaid and private insurance, along with about $2.5 million a year in donations and grants, according to Philanthropic Research Inc.

It is a fact that spiritual care counselors are being denied the right to openly acknowledge God. The United States Constitution guarantees the freedom to openly express one's religious beliefs without prejudice. Is America on its way to becoming a socialist nation?

Rev. Mirta M. Signorelli, MA., Ph.D.